The Art of Narrative

FRIDA C. RUNDELL, PhD, LPC

*To Ian, Helen, and Ella,
For the joy, wonder, and inspiration they give me.*

Copyright 2023 by Frida C. Rundell, PhD, LPC

All rights reserved. No part of this book may be reproduced or used in any manner without written permission of the copyright owner except for the use of quotations in a book review. For more information, address: underthedove@hotmail.com

Printed in USA
Imagine That Enterprises, LC
P.O. Box 220843
St. Louis, MO 63122

Book design by Trese Gloriod, idsign@usa.net
Cover art by Gary Lang
Edited by Lynne Lang

Print: 978-0-9723067-3-7
eBook: 978-0-9723067-5-1

10 9 8 7 6 5 4 3 2

The Art of Narrative offers an insightful interpretation of restorative dialogue, very relevant within the educational setting where diversity, equity, and inclusion efforts form an important part of practice reform. In particular, the narrative underpins transformative thinking needed to internalize change in the mindset of those seeking to strengthen understanding of diversity, equity, and inclusion. The book provides helpful guidelines and a systematic approach for guiding leaders across institutions and professions who are invested in the well-being of their teams with an innovative approach toward strengthening cultural diversity, conflict resolution, inclusivity, and harmony.

Nirusha Lachman, PhD
Chair, Department of Clinical Anatomy. Professor of Anatomy
Professor of Medical Education. Joint Appointment: Department of Surgery,
Division of Plastic Surgery
Mayo Clinic

The Art of Narrative is a pragmatic resource that draws on evidence-informed strategies to assist practitioners with actionable facilitation skills through intentional questions. These structured questions center the facilitation on restorative practices and circle rituals. For example, the questions put forth around scaffolding narrative enable professionals to help others make meaning out of the relations in their lives. These structured questions provide the basis of positive change in the clients that seek professional support.

Daniel F. Perkins, PhD
Professor of Family and Youth Resiliency and Policy
Pennsylvania State University

An easy to read guide for anyone who wishes to increase their facilitation skills and develop thought-provoking questions that invite insights and meaningful conversation.

Joanne Keith, PhD, Professor Emerita
Human Development and Family Studies
Michigan State University

Contents

Foreword 6
Introduction 7

PART ONE

Chapter 1: What is Post-Modern Thinking? 9
Chapter 2: A Systemic Understanding of Restorative Relationships 11
Chapter 3: Narrative Intentions 23
Chapter 4: Stories that Heal 28
Chapter 5: Externalizing Conversations 30
Chapter 6: Positional Maps: Thickening Conversations 33
Chapter 7: The Story: How Meaning is Deconstructed 36
Chapter 8: Deconstructing: Exploring Impact
on Self, Relationships, and Work 40
Chapter 9: Using Sparkling or Unique Moments
Towards a Preferred Narrative 44

PART TWO

Thickening Our Stories: Witness and Community 49
Chapter 10: Re-Authoring Conversations 51
Chapter 11: Re-Membering Conversations 57
Chapter 12: Scaffolding Conversations 60
Chapter 13: Compassionate Witnessing 64
Chapter 14: Documentation, Letter Writing, Arts, and Nature 72
Chapter 15: Co-vision and Co-research 76
Chapter 16: Definitional Ceremonies, Rituals, and Ceremonies 80
Chapter 17: Ethics 83
Glossary of Narrative Terms 90
Appendix A: Externalizing Questions 96
Appendix B: Distress Scale 98
Appendix C: Exercises for Practitioners 99
Afterword: Affirmation & Reflection in Facilitation Skills 102
Resources 107

Foreword

It is my hope that *The Art of Narrative* is a welcome resource for those wishing to deepen their facilitation skills by structuring questions that align with restorative practices within circle processes. Each concept introduced within the chapters is meant to be read, then practiced before moving on to learn what the next chapter contains. Treat each chapter as a building block for the next. The book describes conversational ideas and practices that originate from narrative therapy. Each chapter requires time and space to understand its effectiveness, so take your time and enjoy the journey as it unfolds for you, the reader.

The Art of Narrative is focused on inspiring practitioners in the field of restorative practices to consider different ways of thickening stories. Since narrative facilitation does not give advice, the preference is to thicken the story, allowing the emotional brain to have time to assimilate and accommodate new information. This allows decision-making to come from the storyteller and not the facilitator. The facilitator invites scaffolding questions that bring new insights for the storyteller to discover.

I take great delight in teaching and consulting with others using narrative facilitation processes. My passion for narrative has influenced thousands of students in using these processes and finding significance in meeting the needs of the community.

F. C. Rundell

Frida C. Rundell, Founding Professor
International Institute for Restorative Practices (IIRP)

Introduction

The purpose of this book is to assist facilitators in any discipline who wish to embrace a post-modern paradigm of facilitation. **Post-modern** will be defined and practitioners will be shown how different it is from modern facilitation. The terminology is different in narrative facilitation, so refer to the glossary at the back of the book.

The book is divided into two parts:

Part One introduces the post-modern perspective of working with clients (this could include students, family members, workers, and even working with management). Narrative maps and questions are available to anyone who wishes to improve their questioning skills. However, it does mean you need to change your mindset from trying to "fix the situation" to allowing clients the space to explore their own story. This part of storytelling requires listening and tracking the words clients use more often or occasionally. It is called the **landscape of events** or happenings. There are three specific narrative maps to assist facilitators in doing this: **externalizing maps, positioning maps,** and **unique moments** or **sparkling moment maps**. The first sharing of a story is known as the landscape of events, or happenings. It represents a single person's story of understanding.

Part Two introduces narrative facilitators to building a double story of meaning in their practice. This means that they begin exploring the impact a client's story has had on their present life. Some maps enrich the story. They range from **re-authoring conversations** to **re-membering conversations, silent circles, affirmation circles, listening circles, compassionate witnessing circles,** and **definitional ceremonies,** where using art, music, writing, and other **creative methods** may enrich the story. These processes of thickening a story include witnesses and community providing thoughtful reflections of the storyteller's reality. The thickening process of a story allows the left and right hemispheres of the brain to integrate understanding and insight that may otherwise be lost. Another purpose is to heal the stuck parts of one's story to be released and bring joy to living in the present.

Co-vision, an alternative to supervision, invites small groups to share and practice skills in questioning processes. Post-modern narrative work and facilitation ask clients to give back to society what they have learned about themselves. The ethics of "**taking it back**" indicates that your own story may be the healing of someone else's story.

Enjoy the narrative process. Take your time by practicing what is presented in each chapter before moving on.

PART ONE

CHAPTER 1
What is Post-Modern Thinking?

Storytelling in the twenty-first century challenges us to listen more intentionally with compassion and to build relationships through storytelling. This material will familiarize readers with how to weave together post-modern thinking, restorative practices, and narrative processes in a way that brings hope for the future.

Defining a Post-Modern Paradigm

The twenty-first century introduced a new phase in our thinking. We changed from diagnosis and expert knowledge to acknowledging that people have different realities. This premise poses advantages within communities that require tolerance for differences and the ability to embrace inclusion and equity. The challenge is in implementing this reality into our daily lives. This is the post-modern phase of twenty-first-century thinking.

To understand post-modernism, we need to unpack how modernist thinking embraced and honored expert knowledge over common human reasonableness. During this time, diagnosis became popularized, but in the field of human services, this role was owned by a select few people. Post-modernism, however, invited a social constructionist worldview, where ownership of power, knowledge, and the "truth" is invested in individuals and is encouraged to stay with them. Those of us trained in the expert model are challenged by individuals holding their truth; this changes how we have conversations with humans while respecting their right to their truth. When working with people in relationship building, experts and individuals are encouraged to allow time for awareness and transparency of information before making decisions. Placing everyone on equal footing requires resetting our mindset by understanding the basic premise of post-modern thinking outlined by Freedman and Combs (1996). The premise helps guide facilitators in grappling with how realities are socially constructed and uses language that allows us to organize and maintain our lives through stories. Each person's reality becomes their truth. We will discuss the impact of each premise:

- Realities are socially constructed
- Realities are constituted through language
- Realities are organized and maintained through narrative
- There is no essential truth

As we move into allowing space for single or dominant stories, we allow the short-term memory to access an event that stands out for the individual. Given time with subsequent stories, changes in the social and emotional telling will access different information. Single stories need to be fully explored before moving to preferred stories. A facilitator's challenge is learning to trust the neural pathways of the brain to do the work of transformation. We all wish to be solution-focused and try to "fix it." Instead, we should learn to stay in the "now."

Narrative Question for Personal Growth:

- When does your expert knowledge get in the way of staying with another person's story?

CHAPTER 2
A Systemic Understanding of Restorative Relationships

> *"'Human being' is more a verb than a noun.
> Each of us is unfinished, a work in progress."*
>
> (Rachel Naomi Remen, 1996)

The field of restorative practices, as a social science that builds awareness in relationships, is valuable to understanding human beings. This post-modern perspective honors the sense of belonging, having a voice, and bringing purpose or intention into each individual's life. Sharing this philosophy of respect, reciprocity, and role-modeling enables those engaged in restorative practices to embrace the understanding of the meaning of relationships. This book will explore the relational construct from a systemic perspective where personal regulation of one's affect to reciprocity with others in a proactive stance finally leads to role-modeling for communities on how fair process promotes restorative principles. Restorative practitioners are expected to work within a systemic framework to bring new insights and depth to working with human beings and honoring human dignity.

Diagram 1: A Systemic Understanding of Relationships

Focus of Three R's

1. **Respect for self** (Weingarten, 2003)

2. **Reciprocity is transactional in relationships** (Rundell, 2022)

3. **Role-model processes** with groups and communities

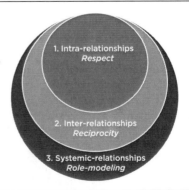

Rundell, F.C. (2022).

We must embrace emotional intelligence by expanding our understanding of restorative practices within a system. Emotional intelligence can provide new insights. Historian Yuval Harari (2019) stated, "Humans have two types of abilities – physical and cognitive" (p. 20). I would argue that emotional intelligence, the capacity to be aware of, control, and express one's emotions and to handle interpersonal relationships, is a skill that can bridge these two abilities. Both emotional intelligence and restorative practices need emotional awareness to be operational. Emotional intelligence activates human beings to act with self-respect and reciprocity for others. It also emphasizes the ability to model these exemplary behaviors for our children and youth, who are still developing their physical and cognitive skills.

As a roadmap, emotional intelligence is consistent with the essential needs of humans in civil society, according to John Bailie, then president of International Institute for Restorative Practices (2019):

> The desire to be treated with dignity is fundamental to all human relationships. This desire manifests itself in the need to belong, to have voice, and to exercise agency in one's own life. It is imperative that those interested in the improvement of civil society gain a more complete understanding of their needs. The emerging social science of restorative practices is to provide a framework to communicate the dimensions of human dignity across cultures and disciplines via the language of the social sciences that is testable through experimentation and research. These insights will be essential to the restoration of community and civil society in the twenty-first century (p.13).

Cognitive abilities enable humans to monitor themselves (intra-relationship), negotiate with others (inter-relationship), and process proactive or responsive circles (systemic modeling) with varying degrees of competence. Humans may act with emotional awareness using physical abilities to respond appropriately. This contributes to our individual and collective functioning within society.

Chapter 2

The Intra-Relationship - Self Compassion

As human beings, we move through life from birth to old age, and our awareness evolves from unaware and disempowered at birth to a gradual growth toward awareness and empowerment. However, this emotional awareness of ourselves allows us to move in and out of the witnessing windows with fluidity (see Diagram 2). Knowing how to regulate ourselves becomes the first priority in being restorative.

Diagram 2: Witnessing Windows

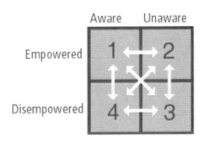

Weingarten K. (2003).

The witnessing windows are permeable spaces that reveal for any self-reflective practitioner where they could be vulnerable. We move in and out of these windows many times during any day. An awareness of how we do this allows us the social and emotional wisdom to respond appropriately when needed. A restorative reflective practice endeavors to maintain respect for self when harmful situations are encountered. Examples of each window will be provided as the intra-relational aspect of restorative practices.

Practitioners are accountable for monitoring and witnessing themselves. Your level of awareness and empowerment becomes your guide. Witnessing windows guide practitioners to recognize where they may find themselves at any moment in time. Each window requires a different response. Tapping into our own personal state of awareness and empowerment will allow us to make different decisions in the care for ourselves (Weingarten, 2003).

As adults, we need to practice self-awareness. If we do not, malpractice and harm may result. Respecting self requires awareness and empowerment and is a comfortable space in which to be. Window 1 allows us to function with ease. Remember, these witnessing windows are fluid and we move in and out of them regularly throughout the day.

Being empowered and unaware in Window 2 signals us as restorative practitioners to ask questions and listen to others to gain awareness of the situation before making any decisions. Harm is more likely to occur if we stay in this window for too long. Malpractice occurs if the empowered practitioner is arrogant and refuses to become aware.

If we find ourselves aware and disempowered, Window 4 acts as a reminder to breathe deeply and take care of our needs before engaging with any critical issues. We may want to avoid situations when experiencing discomfort, but there are times in which witnessing someone's story may cause us discomfort, yet we need to stay present for the sake of that person.

When experiencing moments of unawareness and disempowerment in Window 3, there is a danger of becoming overwhelmed and vulnerable. Therefore, it is essential to take care of self before trying to engage with others. When viewing ourselves in this position, we become vulnerable to influences. This vulnerability warns us to take time out and get rest. Be careful not to make decisions when experiencing this state of helplessness. In monitoring and regulating ourselves, we remain aware and empowered. We make the best decisions in the prefrontal cortex when we have awareness. Awareness is not a single act; it is a continuum of activity that requires continual work on our part as restorative practitioners.

The Inter-Relationship: Engaging with Others

Moving from a balanced self into inter-relational spaces requires a higher level of complexity. *Reciprocity* requires awareness and safety. The

Relational Care Ladder illuminates the competencies that allow spaces where belonging, voice, and agency meet (see Diagram 3). As we move to the inter-relationship framework, the use of the Relational Care Ladder helps us identify others' needs and to establish competencies in which their needs may be met appropriately. Intentional reciprocity propels us to continually check which rungs of the ladder are missing.

Moving from intra-relational to inter-relational aspects of systemic relationships encourages reciprocity with others. Developing relationships means we are fulfilling human needs. The Relational Care Ladder (Diagram 3) addresses these developmental needs by recognizing four rungs of the ladder: structure, nurture, engagement, and challenge. The rungs identify processes that provide the human needs of safety, awareness, feelings, and empowerment, respectively. Human beings flourish when these competencies are met. Conversely, when these competencies are unmet, we become imbalanced in one way or another, resulting in feelings of insecurity and the realization that something is missing. Consequently, over-compensating or isolating behaviors will arise.

Diagram 3: The Relational Care Ladder

Client Needs		Competencies to be used.
Empowerment	CHALLENGE	Competence, Mastery, Play.
Feelings	ENGAGEMENT	Joy of Companionship, Attunement, Now Moments.
Awareness	NURTURE	Security, Self Worth, Stress Reduction.
Safety	STRUCTURE	Safety, Organization, Regulation.

Rundell, F.C. (2021).

Fortunately, in life, different environments may meet different levels of needs at various times. If the home is not safe, school may provide the competency of safety and nurturing, as might friends or colleagues outside the home. For some individuals, the duration, intensity, and frequency of unmet needs may be pervasive. Severe impacts of that kind change the internal chemistry of the body, resulting in a reactionary impulse to find any external stimuli. Behaviors become inappropriate and harmful, not only to the individual but also to others around such a person. This systemic ripple effect is where restorative practices may be useful in understanding the different rungs that promote repairing such harm.

Further discussion about using the restorative questions and the continuum of care can guide us in making restorative decisions. Often, we neglect the rungs for structure and nurture to feel the challenge. As human beings, our needs range from relative safety to awareness of self and others, to expressing feelings, to empowering ourselves and others. We recognize that we may burn out if we continually operate at a challenge rung (empowerment) without continual maintenance of structure (safety) and nurture (awareness). This is a dynamic process where change happens at different times and in different situations.

The rungs of the ladder form the framework of relationship building. Think of a baby that needs to be kept safe while the mother acknowledges the gurgles and sounds and cuddles her little one. Children, youth, and adults need affirming statements within safe surroundings to recognize their self-worth. Offering statements of worthiness in quiet spaces regulates the sensory input and calms individuals in distress. Changing the surroundings to support someone who is hyper-aroused is essential in order to reach the higher rungs of the ladder. Practicing breathing strategies reduces alerts from the amygdala and restores calmness.

Furthermore, affirmations and acknowledgments go a long way in making someone feel seen and valued. Therefore, these practices should become consistent and predictable in promoting stability and nurturing. Also, grounding and awareness are essential needs in any restorative work.

Establishing the first two rungs of the ladder brings calm and worthiness. In addition, engaging in a conversation where feelings are shared becomes easier. Levine (2015) claimed that providing time allows the prefrontal lobe to make sound decisions. Once this is achieved, challenges may be presented with insight and understanding.

How does harm occur within relationships? When our needs as children, youth, and adults, are not met, harm results. It is up to the adults, who are aware, to implement appropriate measures to provide competencies that address unmet needs. The needs for safety, awareness, and expressing feelings are critical for human dignity. These restorative ingredients invite a sense of empowerment. Often, individuals operate at the challenge level, where they empower themselves, and many times, these individuals forget to do daily structure and nurture rung activities to ground themselves. If sufficient structure or nurture rungs are not maintained daily, these individuals may experience burnout or emotional collapse when difficult and harmful events occur.

Reciprocity is the give-and-take in relationships. People meet each other's needs in different ways within communities. Circles can play a role in meeting some of these needs. Various types of circles include: proactive, responsive, listening, or compassionate witnessing. The different structures of each circle create a sense of safety, nurturing, engagement, and/or challenge.

The Systemic-Relationship: Organizational Best Practices

Entering the macro-level of systemic relationships invites an overview of how restorative practices influence intra- and inter-systems. Role modeling is where restorative leadership engages with communities and businesses in processes that promote belonging, voice, and agency (Bailie, 2019). It requires consistency, predictability, and unconditional regard for self and others to effectively impact individuals and groups.

The ideal of doing things *with* others becomes the mantra.

Diagram 4 illustrates how organizations, businesses, or schools that are neglectful (*not*) of individuals' needs tend to experience different levels of exploitation. Harmful environments ignore normal human needs yet expect high performance. Communities develop toxic behaviors to meet their needs. Neglecting and ignoring human needs usually causes gaps to develop at different levels. For example, neglecting a child can affect that person into their adulthood. Also, employers who does not provide the appropriate equipment during a pandemic for essential workers may endanger the workers and essentially invite the deaths that could result. Then, a leader of a country who ignores the needs of that country creates chaos and discontent. Thus, structure and support are key elements for individuals to experience a sense of security.

Any system or organization that micro-manages its employees creates punitive (*to*) ways to maintain its rules and boundaries. The military provides an excellent example of doing things *to* others. Businesses and organizations that micro-manage their employees impede personal initiative and self-motivation. The inflexibility of a system impacts the participants in two possible ways: (a) they either respond with loyalty or (b) leave as a rebel.

When organizations or communities are permissive (*for*), they tend to over-protect, causing individuals to feel entitled. Generally, the organization's system fails to provide appropriate boundaries and expectations to guide employees. The tendency is to emotionally lock individuals into a tacit understanding of loyalty and expectation. As a result, they create a populace with no awareness of social norms outside of their environment; these individuals have unrealistic expectations of others. Their level of entitlement is apparent, and they do not display awareness of self or others. Rather, they tend to change their expectations, dependent on mood or emotions. This over-indulged attitude may result in certain inappropriate expectations.

The organization or system that creates a restorative approach (*with*) provides appropriate norms and boundaries that empower belonging, engagement, and purpose. Everyone needs clear and appropriate structure, boundaries, and expectations. Social awareness provides a balance between self and others. Restorative processes encourage and support participants to actively maintain respect for each other, with leadership modeling regular check-ins and other rituals for accountability, where all voices can be heard. This is a continual dynamic state.

When systemic relationships move to organizations and businesses, leadership and employees are required to role-model relational competencies. Providing expectations for accountability while maintaining support and self-worth can challenge role-modeling. The *Social Discipline Window* (see Diagram 4) initially used by IIRP has been adapted to reflect the tension between accountability and support. Behaviors and actions must demonstrate a sense of belonging while allowing everyone to voice their feelings and intentions. Intentionality guides purpose and is the restorative maxim of doing things *with* others, creating greater satisfaction in relationships (Bailie, 2019).

Diagram 4: Social Discipline Window

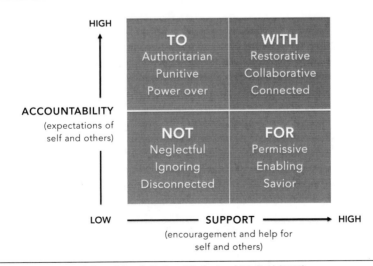

Adapted by Abrams, G.B. and Smull, B. from Wachtel and McCold (2000).

In summary, repairing harm and imbalance in our lives must begin within ourselves. Establishing *respect for self* should be a priority. Once we can regulate our own affect (how we are internally affected) in situations, we can engage with others respectfully. Moreover, *reciprocity with others* allows proactive engagement in the well-being of others. Intentional reciprocity brings awareness and empowerment to both parties in the relationship. The preparation for human beings to enter into reciprocity happens in ever-increasing concentric circles, first within the family, extended family, then in school, and organizations, where role modeling changes relationships with meaning.

Restorative processes identify the key needs of belonging, having a voice, and agency in meeting human needs. Consistent and predictable practices should be commonly used by practitioners (e.g., check-in, check-out, welcome, and goodbye circles). Demonstrating how to establish norms that guide behaviors and practices is another valuable process. It is important to include all employees, utilizing the fair process components of explanation, engagement, and expectation clarity. Fundamentally, role modeling with employees, students, staff, communities, and parents invites them to follow a restorative paradigm.

Respect, reciprocity, and role modeling—speaks to the systematic development of restorative practices and how our map of consciousness may change when we consider these factors in our daily work. Learning to regulate our own emotional energy and expectations begins the journey. The emotional awareness is constantly in flux, is dynamic, changing moment to moment, and context to context. *Weingarten's Witnessing Windows* guide us to be vigilant as practitioners. Meeting the needs of other human beings encourages restorative practitioners to address gaps in the Relational Care Ladder and provide necessary competencies. When using restorative practices within organizations, schools, communities, and businesses, it is necessary to model practices exemplary of a *"with"* perspective, as shown in the Social Discipline Window.

A systemic understanding invites us to be accountable and supportive of ourselves, others, and our organizations in proactive and responsive ways. Relationships require maintenance, sustainability, consistency, predictability, and unconditional regard to flourish. Self-respect, reciprocity with others, and role modeling processes complete the human need for safety, awareness, feelings, and empowerment. Once these are established, we can empower individuals, groups, and society to face challenges that uphold human dignity.

Dominant Stories Deconstructed

Leo Marks (1920-2001) wrote:

The life that I have
Is all that I have
And the life that I have
Is yours.
The love that I have
Of the life that I have
Is yours, and yours, and yours.
A sleep I shall have
Yet death will be but a pause,
For the peace of my years
In the long green grass
Will be yours, and yours, and yours.

Life experiences form part of our DNA as human beings, and influence our stories. Initially, narrative facilitators listen with intention. Using open-ended questions, we learn how to use externalization and positional and unique maps that expand on meaning, effects, and effects of the effects of any issues the client wishes to discuss (see Diagram 5). When a story is first told, it often stays with the landscape of events, which is known as the *dominant story*. Some moments contradict or highlight a different theme or pattern from the dominant story. Catching those blips when listening makes use of *unique moments*. Essentially, listening intentionally demands a process founded on separating the deed from the doer.

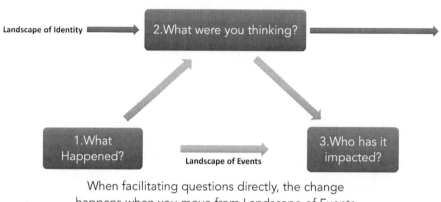

Diagram 5: Landscapes of Events and Identity

When facilitating questions directly, the change happens when you move from Landscape of Events to Landscape of Identity.

Rundell, F.C. (2022).

Moving any descriptive adjectives (e.g., angry, worried, anxious) to use them as nouns (the anger, the worry, the anxiety) helps to move the issue outside of the person. In this way, we separate the deed from the doer. Asking questions that move back and forth between the first order of cybernetics, known as the *landscape of events/actions*, and the second order of cybernetics, known as the *landscape of identity/consciousness*, allows the storyteller to have the freedom to move from a stuck pattern to view other options. This is the primary intention of a narrative facilitator who listens restoratively (see Diagram 5).

Narrative Question for Personal Growth:

- How does the "Parent" (Control) in you show up and why?

CHAPTER 3
Narrative Intentions

Storytelling is at the heart of narrative inquiry. Five common themes in the post-modern social construction of stories acknowledge that (White, 2007):
1. Power is both personal and structural.
2. Individuals have the right to participate.
3. Social change is inevitable, whether personally or collectively, or both.
4. Knowledge in a story could be empirical and constructed.
5. Communication and dialogue are critically important.

Stories have a beginning, a middle, and an end. In today's world, the idea of evidence-based learning has become essential in gaining funding for research projects, which emphasizes beginnings and endings. Yet in a narrative the *middle* is where many variations within a story exist. This is lost in the modern-day pursuit of evidence-based learning. How do we cultivate the middle, which is messy and allows ambiguities to exist? When thickening a story, we seek meaning that may not fit the dominant story. However, narrative inquiry encourages dialogic conversations that allow us to construct meaning and generate new meanings; it punctuates different levels of experiences with a unique level of understanding. At the same time, it opens the social and emotional parts of the brain, making positive change more viable.

A narrative conversation invites a storyteller to explore and thicken their understanding of their story before entertaining any alternatives. The facilitator's work is to remain curious and function as the non-expert. This does not mean that the facilitator lets "anything go." Instead, the facilitator's intention is to guide questions that zigzag in and out between the landscape of events and the landscape of identity.

Other frameworks, called maps, are used to develop meaning and a sense of purpose. A narrative conversation can be compared to meeting at a crossroad. Discussions at intersections like this provide freedom and a non-judgmental space, inviting the storyteller to name, claim and reframe their story in the best way possible.

Stories have been the most powerful, innermost part of all cultures and communities since the beginning of time (Duvall & Beres, 2011). Collaboration in mapping the storyteller's story constitutes an important journey. The facilitator has to de-center from self and re-center, staying centered on the storyteller and the story. In the beginning, a historical past is explored through a genogram, an eco-map of connections, and any relevant facts. Validating and empathizing are critical during the dominant story phase. Hearing and thickening a story from a single story to a double story takes time and maybe a few sessions. Only then can facilitators begin to challenge the story by exploring its impact on self and others. This is the "messiness" or "middle" of the story that provides different flavors and options. At this point, any unique comments or moments can be used to highlight an alternative pattern or theme, which may be often dismissed or submerged due to the power of the dominant story. Narrative conversations are always interactive. The journey follows the storyteller's preference. Narrative facilitators often ask the following types of questions:

- Could you tell me what you mean by ... ?
- This has me curious. Could you tell me more?
- How is this conversation going for you?
- Should we keep talking about this, or would you be more interested in ... ?
- Is this interesting to you? Is this what we should spend our time talking about?
- I was wondering if you would be more interested in me asking you some more about this or whether we should focus on X, Y, or Z?

Narrative conversations are guided by the interests of those with whom facilitators consult. Basic narrative principles are:
- Approach all clients and communities with respect and non-blaming where the individual or community remains the expert.
- Remember always to separate the problem from the individual. This is done by externalizing the problem and changing the issue to a noun.
- Remain curious and "unknowing," allowing space to deepen the conversation.

There is no one direction to follow in facilitating a storyteller's journey.

The conversation between the storyteller and the facilitator plays a significant role in determining trust and the direction of the conversation. Facilitators provide a structure that creates safety and engagement, and only after the therapeutic alliance has been established can challenges to the dominant story be explored (see The Relational Care Ladder in Chapter 2). Alternative stories may also be referred to as the *preferred reality*.

When facilitators address a client's story, there are different aspects of the story that the facilitator may follow:
- Events
- Across Time
- Linked Sequences
- According to a Plot

Example: A story about my birthday celebrations

Remembering the events of my birthday celebrations could begin when I turned 70 years old, and I chose to have a drumming circle for 25 young people who had been expelled from school. What was I thinking at the time? I thought I was providing a chance for them to experience a fun part of themselves. What did I realize after the event? This activity presented a threat to some students, while others thought it was a chance to skip school work; still, others engaged with enthusiasm.

How was this celebration different from other birthday celebrations?

At 60 years old, I chose to give myself a birthday party. At the time, it was hard work but turned out to be one of the most memorable birthdays I ever had. Friends brought stories that connected them to me and shared them in different conversations. I learned that allowing my friends to share their experiences was most fulfilling.

Was there ever another celebration that gave a similar feeling of satisfaction?

Yes! My 21st birthday was a surprise barbeque with friends and family playing "Some Funny Orchestra," which was funny and goofy but memorable.

Exploring the idea of "birthday celebrations" started with a recent event, where I realized that "*giving to others*" was an important option in planning a birthday celebration. How I might spend future birthdays would be a new and *preferred alternative story*. The realization of giving to others introduced a preferred way to celebrate a birthday.

The Effects of the Dominant Stories

The dominant story of my birthday celebrations will not only affect me in the present but will also have implications for my future actions. For example, in the future, I may consider including friends who might not require much work and avoid celebrating with students without asking them ahead of time. I enjoy surprises that include special people in my life. Letting others know about my preference would be important. These impacts could be explored even further.

The same process of thickening a preferred story may begin with exploring the impacts on different significant people and environments. Again, the richness in the narrative is in thickening stories. Narrative curiosity increases the ability to move a dominant story to thicker connections with the impact and the attributes we attach from our past to our present. Some we prefer to diminish in value, while others we honor the strengths with which they embrace us. Over time, the links between past, present, and future will shape new insights that powerfully impact our lives. In this way, we begin re-authoring our lives.

Narrative Questions for Personal Growth:

- With whom have you recently spent time?
- Have you remained curious about an event or celebration with this person?

CHAPTER 4

Stories that Heal

"Truth is so much harder than fiction ... What is the point of trying to put down on paper emotions that are too complex, too huge, too overwhelming to be confined by an alphabet?"

(Picoult, 2013, p. 357)

When people consult with us to facilitate their journey, our first premise is to understand how they use words to describe their lives. Clients use language and stories to describe themselves that identify their values and beliefs, which are pivotal when deconstructing what the words or stories mean.

As facilitators, we begin hearing thin descriptions of the story. During the thickening and expanding of the story, we use our narrative ear to uncover unique stories that do not fit with the dominant story. By thickening a unique story, the facilitator draws attention to alternative ways that may be possible for the storyteller/client. Exploring rich descriptions of the alternative story allows an opportunity for empathy and sharing. Brown (2015) discussed how narrative conversations build bonds that become healing alliances. Vulnerability works like a gauge between shame and empathy. Allowing compassion, non-judgment, "not knowing," and uncertainty are important processes when facilitators listen to storytellers/clients.

Diagram 6: Vulnerability

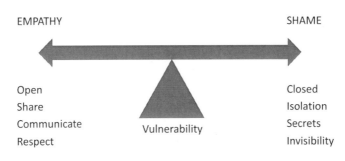

Brown, B. (2015).

Vulnerability is one's choosing a space in which to feel safe. This can happen when the witnesses to a story provide acknowledgment and empathy, which can be felt by the storyteller.

Narrative Questions for Personal Growth:

- When and where have you felt affirmed and acknowledged?
- What did that feeling remind you of?

CHAPTER 5
Externalizing Conversations

"The initiative of youth and the experience of the old each have equal value." (Brian Stevenson)

One of the key pathways in narrative facilitation is that of separating the deed from the doer. This road requires the facilitator to turn adjectives/adverbs into nouns. Changing a descriptive word into a noun creates space to examine the issue as an entity outside of the self. Additionally, objectivity within a conversation allows the storyteller to examine the issue through a different lens.

My mother would not tolerate cursing and swearing. As an eight-year-old, I had never heard curse words. When Johnny and Kenny, our neighborhood kids, would visit and play on the swings and slides with us as children, we heard some new words. I tried out a few of these choice words when I got back home, only to find my mother calling me to the pantry, chopping up chilis, and rubbing my mouth with them. The burning was intolerable. My grandmother who saw my pain silently called me back into the pantry and fed me dry bread to take away the burn. My mother failed to explain to me that these words were curse words. I was confused by my mother's response but felt compassion from my grandmother.

The following is an example of a narrative facilitator (NF) exploring the landscape of identity/consciousness with a storyteller (ST):

NF: How does intolerable pain impact you?

ST: I get confused and feel guilty but don't know why. The severe punishment taught me to avoid hot food like curries and anything to do with chilis. A conversation with me would have clarified the situation and provided me with a different understanding than what has been a lifetime impression. I learned I could not share ideas with my mother; however, my grandmother became my confidante.

NF: How has harsh punishment impacted you?

ST: To this day, I still use a few curse words but cannot eat hot food. I rebel verbally against anyone who uses severe punishment toward me or anyone I love. Fairness and understanding are extremely important to me.

The easiest way to change a conversation into externalization is to move the descriptor and personify it as if it is an object or person.

When I am angry, speak to the anger or Mr. Anger.

When I am frustrated, speak to the frustration or Freaky Frustration.

When I am confused, speak to the confusion or Cloudy Confusion.

Remember to always allow the storyteller to name their own noun. Having the power to choose allows the limbic part of the brain to own it. Naming it and claiming it is particularly motivating for the storyteller. The name chosen becomes part of the reframing process. This is necessary fuel for neurons to fire before the storyteller can talk objectively about an issue.

Additionally, the ability to move the feeling word into a noun allows the storyteller a space to examine the concept in a broader sense. Using the positional stops allows facilitators to access a different landscape of identity/consciousness.

- What does it mean?
- How do you allow _____ into your life?

- How does this impact you?
- When have you gotten the better of _____ in your life?
- How does it impact others in your life?

Refer to the exercises in Appendix A for practicing externalization processes. Have fun doing this.

In summarizing externalization, we, as narrative facilitators, continually seek to externalize descriptions the storyteller holds true to self and to uncover and understand alternative perspectives. This is how we *separate the deed from the doer*.

Narrative Questions for Personal Growth:

- When did you let Anger or Anxiety come in through your front door?
- What did you do to entertain it?

CHAPTER 6
Positional Maps: Thickening Conversations

Storytelling addresses the opportunity to be culturally curious about the storyteller's context and how their experience has formed their perceptions of life. The insight promotes inter-connectedness across cultural boundaries and broadens our tolerance for differences in relationships.

In post-modern thinking, we socially construct our lives through stories. According to Freedman and Combs (1996), "Our realities are socially constructed through language, organized and maintained through narrative, and there is no essential truth" (p. 22) except to the storyteller. Our imaginations may allow us to create and re-invent ourselves at any time. The questions you ask about the way in which the experience impacts the identity, or level of consciousness, are the ones that bring about change. Opening and thickening the story should be purposeful. The change happens first in the limbic part of the brain, where you allow no judgment, only freedom of expression. This is referred to as the landscape of events/actions (first order) or the "near experience" (White, 1996). Then as you pose abstract questions relating to self and others, the landscape of identity/consciousness (second order) is explored. Neurologically, the neural pathways allow the logical brain to make connections it previously had been unable to make.

For this reason, narrative facilitation is never prescriptive but rather exploratory. Through exploring different relationship scenarios or options within an issue, myelination (thickening of the neurons) occurs. The beauty is in the fact that the storyteller discovers solutions and insights, thus enabling change at a far deeper level.

Remember that stories have a beginning, middle, and end. Narrative facilitation spends most of its time in the middle, thickening the story. Narrative inquiry is best at exploring options, where single or dominant stories are invited to become double or thickened stories. Narrative facilitation intentionally asks storytellers questions that move from a dominant story to alternative stories. An extremely useful framework or map for a facilitator is the process of externalization and positional mapping. These maps may be used with the dominant story and alternative stories.

White (1996) used narrative stories and questions to assist us in reaching that preferred reality using positional maps or questions.

Stage 1. What is the problem or issue on your mind?
- a. What is the meaning of the problem?
- b. Is there a name you would give this meaning?

Stage 2. What are the effects of this dominant story?
- a. On your life?
- b. On your relationships?
- c. On your work?

Stage 3. What are the effects of the effects of this dominant story?
- a. On your life?
- b. On your relationships?
- c. On your work?

Stage 4. What is your preferred story?
- a. How would that be possible?
- b. Have there been times when you felt things were improving in your life?

When the facilitator is deconstructing any event, or opportunity from the past, present, or future, new insights enrich the event and allow aspects to thicken. Consider these questions:

- Which values enriched the story and made a difference for the present or future?
- What unnamed background assumptions make this event a teachable moment?
- What realizations became evident and explained how people were behaving?
- What are some of the taken-for-granted ways that give life to the problem?

Once the storyteller has unpacked the dominant story, the alternative or preferred reality is explored with the same positional map. The preferred or alternative story requires the same set of intentional questions. Once the meaning of words is explored and established, this impact on the storyteller and the context come into play.

Remember, it is a journey. You may pick up and stop at any point. When traveling, you stop for a breakfast break or a rest stop. This allows you and the storyteller to enjoy the view and spend some time appreciating little things. Take time to do this when using narrative facilitation. The conversation is about building a relationship that brings beauty and insight into the richness of life. In the next two chapters, we will explore the specific aspects of each positional map.

Narrative Questions for Personal Growth:

- What is most difficult for you in changing a triggering event at work?
- What support do you wish to invite in?

CHAPTER 7

The Story: How Meaning is Deconstructed

Keep in mind that as you deconstruct the first step in a positional map, a problem is not always necessary. There may be something on the person's mind that needs to be verbalized in order to seek clarity. It may be an emotion that was experienced or an issue that surfaced. Engaging intentionally with whatever is presented is appropriate in narrative work.

What's On Your Mind?

Joining your storyteller at the beginning of your session is important. When first starting, provide a clear understanding of your expectations and goals as a narrative facilitator. Informal conversation is often helpful in taking the edge off any anxiety the storyteller may have. Many times, it provides useful contextual knowledge.

A distress scale is a useful indicator. It indicates how emotional the storyteller is by using a number (see Appendix B). Mindful exercises at the start of each conversation are another option. Grounding a scattered storyteller before starting helps the person stay in the "now." Any other ritual that honors your storyteller is appropriate. For example:
- What is the meaning of the problem?
- Is there a name you would give this meaning?

Listen carefully to the words the storyteller uses. Never assume you know the meaning of words. Asking what a word means presents an ideal opportunity to ask respectfully and follow a deeper understanding within the conversation.

Chapter 7

See the example here with the narrative facilitator (NF):

Jimmy: I suffer from depression and need help.

NF: What does depression mean to you?

Jimmy: Oh, it means I am always sad and negative about life. There is a wall between me and others. I am never happy.

NF: So what name, object, or animal would you give to this collection of words: sad, negative, a wall, and unhappy?

Jimmy: The first thing that came to me was the character, "Eeyore," from *Winnie-the-Pooh*.

NF: What impact has Eeyore had on your personal life?

Jimmy: Well, I don't sleep well. I wake up tired. Work takes a lot of effort.

NF: When work takes so much effort, what happens to your productivity?

Jimmy: I have already received several written warnings that I need to be more focused, but I don't care.

NF: What is making you vulnerable to Eeyore at work?

Jimmy: I think it is because I have stayed in this job for so long, and there is no hope for any promotion.

NF: What does hope look like to you?

Jimmy: Hope would mean that I have friends at work to talk to. I would be earning enough to pay my bills. I would also be using some of my creative potential to bring new ideas to the workplace.

NF: Tell me about a time when you got the better of Eeyore?

Jimmy: When I was at college, I had a group of three friends. We were so good for each other. We used our drawing and technical skills to design a machine that could eject tennis balls for practicing tennis. It was the coolest thing. One thing we did not have was the business acumen to go for a patent.

NF: That is truly creative and having friends to share it with. You could have made money on that. Did you ever share the idea with someone who has the knowledge of how to patent it?

Jimmy: Yes! We did share it with someone who actually stole our idea and patented it under his name. We were extremely naive in those days.

NF: Would you say that to beat Eeyore you would need to consider bringing friendships, creativity, and better pay rates into your life? How would Eeyore experience that?

Jimmy: I think Eeyore would be shocked and surprised. It is certainly something to consider.

NF: If you think about friendships, creativity, and better pay, what phrase, animal, place, or word describes them in your mind?

Jimmy: A Contented Cat.

NF: I am Eeyore, and I want you to sculpt me.

Jimmy: You are on all four legs, with your head down, sitting on the back legs, eyes closed.

NF: Wow! This does feel sad and lonely. I can feel the depression. Now I want you to sculpt me as a Contented Cat.

Jimmy: You are on all four legs but playfully prancing around with other cats and licking your paws every now and then.

NF: This feels so different to Eeyore. I feel light and lively. What small movement do I need to do from Eeyore to the Contented Cat that could start bringing the change you want toward the Contented Cat?

Once you have participated in the deconstructing of what it means, ask the storyteller to give it a name. This process removes the intensity of the issue outside of the person telling the story and allows space to unpack it objectively. Separating the deed from the doer means you have externalized it. In the example, I used my own body to sculpt the experience of both images (e.g., Eeyore and The Contented Cat). This allows for a contrast that is easily experienced. The difference allows the storyteller to recognize the steps needed to move to an alternate story, encouraging one small movement to allow contemplation of possible change in the future. Once this has been deconstructed, you are ready to explore the impact on the person's life, work, and relationships. In the next chapter, we will explore how to follow the impact on different relationships.

Narrative Questions for Personal Growth:

- Who are the people you seek to please?
- What happens when pleasing does not work?

CHAPTER 8

Deconstructing: Exploring Impact on Self, Relationships, and Work

Asking questions helps storytellers understand explicitly how the dominant issue has impacted their identity and is one of the most valuable aspects of narrative inquiry. These conversations are powerful moments of awareness when exploring anything from relationships to dreams and hopes.

The type of questions used to explore the dominant and alternative or preferred stories may range from asking about the impact on:

a. Yourself
b. Your relationships
c. Your work/school

Each exploration will provide a time sequence that moves from effect and then to the effect of the effect.

Example 1: Procrastination's impact/effect on self and work

"Procrastination" leads to trust issues within self and among others that then can result in a distorted identity and possible dismissal.

SELF

> NF: How does procrastination impact you?
>
> Maria: I get disappointed in myself and think I am not capable.
>
> NF: Where does disappointment lead you?
>
> Maria: Oh! In everything, I now just follow what others dictate, and I have no opinions of my own.

Chapter 8

WORK/OTHERS

NF: How does procrastination affect your relationship with your boss?

Maria: My boss does not trust me to complete any task without continually reminding me.

NF: What impact does not trusting have on you?

Maria: I get annoyed with the continual reminders. I am not a child to be treated like that.

NF: What happens if and when you show that annoyance toward him?

Maria: I think he would dismiss me.

NF: If you are dismissed from your job, how will that impact your relationship at home?

Maria: I would be so ashamed and devastated.

NF: Has the lack of trust brought you any further realizations about your future in the company? What is it you would see that you need to change?

A positional map provides guidelines that invite the storyteller to unpack the issue by first deconstructing the meaning of words. Michael White (1996) encouraged the narrative facilitator to trace the impact of that story. Tracing the story requires exploration of the effects of the externalized name within different contexts. The intention is to keep the positional map in the back of your mind as a facilitator. Listening carefully to the words the storyteller uses and tracking them in a chain reaction broadens the understanding and the actual issue or theme. The last example demonstrated how intentional listening tracks a story.

Identify the problem using externalization or personification, then expose it for the tricks and tactics that serve to confuse the storyteller. These beliefs make the storyteller vulnerable to the problem and allow the problem to take over the dominant stage of their life. In the end, this dominant story, with its plan, gets laid open for the storyteller to evaluate.

The Positional Map Stages:

Step 1: What issue is on the storyteller's mind? Explore what it means.

Step 2: What is the effect (impact) of the issue?

Step 3: What is the effect (impact) of the effect (impact)?

Step 4: Is there something you would like to change or adjust for yourself?

Step 5: Was there a time when you experienced something entirely different?

Asking Step 5 invites the storyteller to experience a sparkling moment or a preferred reality.

At this point, you have prepared the storyteller emotionally to contemplate a life change regarding the story. Bringing awareness to the storyteller through questions works with how human beings' emotional and social brain accommodates new information. Neuroscience shows how this is a far more effective way of changing behavior (Levine, 2015; Porges, 2011).

The greatest achievement in narrative inquiry is when the storyteller has separated from the behavior and can visualize the impact of the behavior on self, other relationships, work, and home.

Chapter 8

You are now ready to help your storyteller thicken the story using a sparkling moment or a preferred reality. To do this, you will repeat the same positional map questions using the preferred or alternative story. The difference will pertain to their preference for the future. Enjoy exploring the landscape of identity or consciousness. The following chapter will explain how to extract the sparkling moments in your storyteller's life.

Narrative Question for Personal Growth:

A daily practice helps to regulate you as a narrative practitioner.

- How often do you take time to check in with your body for 12 minutes?

CHAPTER 9
Using Sparkling or Unique Moments Towards a Preferred Narrative

We have unpacked the dominant story and traced its sequence and timing. Now we are ready to hear any unique or sparkling moments that contradict the dominant story. The narrative facilitator will use the same treatment as with the dominant story by moving the storyteller toward embracing those sparkling moments with more intensity and depth (Refer to the positional map with the exploration of a preferred story). This enables the storyteller to choose, at a later stage, an alternative or preferred personal belief or desire. Once the groundwork is complete in broadening the impact of the story, the storyteller is asked whether they wish to continue in the same way or if there is a desire to change. Here, any sparkling moments or blips on the screen become visible. The storyteller may only wish to make a few life changes or choose to make some major changes. The goal of narrative is to explore options that open up the emotional brain to be curious and willing to explore options before making any decisions. The major question that is asked after unpacking the dominant story is, "When were you able to trick _____ (the externalized theme) and not allow it to have the upper hand?"

Sparkling moments or unique outcomes manifest themselves in a variety of ways. The landscape of action/events with the landscape of identity/consciousness questions zigzag in and out of the storyteller's story to establish the significance of the sparkling or unique moments. Exploring ideas, assumptions, and beliefs that have been taken for granted are explored using the same positional maps as we used before. The difference is that we are shifting from the problem to considering a possible change. This may often be about a forgotten moment experienced in the past. Exploring the meaning of words or phrases

Chapter 9

and preferred externalizations all help objectify the sparkling moment. The storyteller eases into new possibilities within the positional map and a scaffolding process.

The questions range from effect to effect of the effect. The same questioning skills used in the dominant story are used for this questioning. Stories survive through the telling and retelling of special moments. There is power in tracing the sparkling moment and helping the storyteller to connect the dots. Lives get lived by the dominant themes of a story. The purpose of tracing a unique story is to find the varying effects of forgotten parts of the storyteller's life that have brought them hope and joy.

Eventually, the storyteller may decide the parts of the story to keep and which they wish to minimize. When the facilitator deconstructs any story with the storyteller, the opportunities for new realizations, learnings, and surprises become evident.

Example: A dominant story of the *"Work Habit"* that leads to escaping home to work longer hours.

The impact is that when finally coming home, more arguments and irritability erupt. Once in the past, the couple spent 15 minutes having time together over coffee and sharing the events of the day with each other.

Explore the dominant story on self:

NF: How has the work habit affected you?

Martin: It drives me crazy, and I become short-tempered and irritable when I get home.

NF: When the short-temperedness visits, what happens then?

Martin: I find myself continually wanting to escape from being home. I find outside distractions like working in my garage until late (effect of effect).

Exploring the impact on others:

> NF: How has the work habit affected your relationship?
>
> Martin: I feel compelled to always be busy and not think about things.
>
> NF: Is that driving you further apart or closer to your spouse?
>
> Martin: No, it is driving each of us further apart.
>
> NF: Do you remember a time when it was different between the two of you?

Exploring the sparkling moment:

> Martin: Oh, yes! Two years ago, we used to greet each other at the end of the day with a good long kiss and cuddle then sit down for 15 minutes to drink a cup of coffee. We would share any events from our day with each other.
>
> NF: I noticed how your eyes sparkled as you shared that story with me. What has changed that routine now?
>
> Martin: Having a baby to look after and tend to its needs.
>
> NF: What do you realize you would need to do to bring back some of that sparkle into your life?
>
> Martin: I think I need to ask for 15 minutes after the baby is in bed just for the two of us.

The narrative facilitator makes a note of any sparkling or unique moments. These are referred to later when we start to thicken the story using others who are witnesses to the story. We have covered many different aspects of a story and how narrative questions remain open-ended, zigzagging between first-order (landscape of events) and second-order (landscape of identity) cybernetics. There is a structure to working with someone from meaning to impact, which opens the emotional brain (limbic region) to accommodate new opportunities in their daily living.

Landscape of Actions or Event Questions

Here are some possible questions that could be asked when exploring a unique outcome:

- Who was with you when this happened?
- How long ago did this happen?
- How long did this experience last?
- Was this planned, or did it happen by accident?

Landscape of Identity Questions

Some possible questions exploring identity questions:

1. **Desires, Wishes, and Preferences**
   What do you want for your life when you consider what you experienced then?

2. **Personal Values**
   What personal values show up in the incident you just shared?

3. **Relationship Qualities**
   How does this moment explain what you value in the relationship?

4. **Personal Skills and Abilities**
   What did you have to do to make that happen?

5. **Intentions, Motives, Plans, and Purposes**
   Was there any planning or pre-thinking before you allowed yourself to experience this event?

6. **Beliefs and Values**
   Tell me how this speaks to your own personal values or beliefs?

7. **Personal Qualities**
   How does this honor your own personal abilities/skills/knowledge?

In working with a sparkling moment, you facilitate a process of opening the storyteller's mind to alternative ways of being. This is an exciting and beautiful experience for both the storyteller and facilitator. Enjoy the journey. In Part Two, we will explore how thickening the story invites community connection.

Narrative Question for Personal Growth:

- How many hugs did you invite into your life today?

PART TWO

THICKENING OUR STORIES
Witness and Community

The criminal justice system views restorative justice as the opportunity to invite the victim, offender, and community that cares to the circle. This begins the emotional journey of healing.

In mental health and well-being, witnessing one another invites listeners to a circle where belonging and having a voice provide a sense of agency. Moreover, restorative practices underpin the foundation of respect for all humanity and honor human dignity (Bailie, 2019). When we witness other peoples' stories, we thicken the story by grappling with its impact on the storyteller's identity. Witnesses honor the story by using the 5 Cs (see page 50). These invited witnesses may be people known or unknown to the storyteller seeking healing. Circles are not only for harm, as in restorative justice conferences, but also offer a voice for smaller incidents. In such cases, restorative practices advocate for a wide variety of types of circles.

Ask yourself if you can stay with another person's story long enough to connect with curiosity and compassion in order to provide a sense of community. When we listen long enough, our neural pathways generate oxytocin, making us feel safe, loved, and cared for.

Where were you on the 5 Cs?

Connect: When you said ____, I thought/or felt _____.

Curious: You mentioned _____ and I was wondering if_____?

Compassion: I was so struck by your_____.

enCouragement: I'd like to commend you on _____.

Community: As you were telling your story, I thought about where you would have wanted support or thought of telling another person _____.

In narrative inquiry, there are many different ways to thicken a story. We will explore some of these ways. We call them narrative maps. I will introduce you to questions that could assist you in using maps of re-authoring, remembering, scaffolding, compassionate witnessing, listening circles, co-vision, writing and documentation, rituals, and celebration. We will close with ways narrative inquiry addresses ethics. Hopefully, you will benefit and experience a fruitful richness when sharing our humanity in our stories. See the diagrams that unfold the thickness or double story-ing.

The richness in understanding the middle of a story invites history and cultural differences to highlight new insights. We create and accommodate new, creative ideas when we hear another person's story. The process prompts the ability to envisage our potential as humans. It then becomes easier to make changes in our lives, and making our own choice is more likely. Fundamentally, witnessing relationships creates community and empowers change.

CHAPTER 10
Re-Authoring Conversations

The purpose of re-authoring a client's conversation is to "re-develop the subordinate storylines of people's lives" (White, 2007, p. 128). Simply put, White's approach suggested that when a client seeks help, there is a dominant storyline that is problematic in some way for the client. To help the client change their internal narrative and perception, White looked for and solicited stories that were not in line with the dominant storyline, which he referred to as unique outcomes or exceptions (p. 62). This seems synonymous with what Freedman and Combs (1996) called sparkling moments. White explored, developed, or thickened the plot of these exceptions by exploring them through the landscape of identity/consciousness as well as the landscape of action over the past, present, and future. In this way, White was able to draw out new ways of seeing a situation, creating new insights, and inviting new meaning into the client's life. These insights align themselves with a preferred reality.

Narrative questions continuously remain curious. Playing with words and metaphors allows a playfulness that imbues the practitioner with permission to enjoy the storyteller's story as if it were a journey. On a journey, you may stop and view a beautiful sight, take some photos, and honor it. That is where the practitioner's intent should be. Many experiences in life that were beneficial are often blipped over. In re-authoring, we get to enjoy those moments and elevate the experience.

Michael White used the re-authoring narrative map to help his clients find new meanings that overlooked or neglected actions they elicited in the past. White explained that when people seek help, they are more likely to "speak about the history of the problems, predicaments, or dilemmas that have brought them to you" (White, 2007, p. 61). Re-authoring asks the client to step away from the problem that has shaped their identity, and instead, it looks at the actions that contradict who they believe themselves to be. By inviting the client into a conversation that has them re-author their own narrative, practitioners use a series of narrative questions to unpack, open space, and provide new insight into what the important people in their life saw in them.

In re-authoring conversation, the practitioner challenges the client's belief in self. Asking what a special person in their lives most appreciated about them begins the re-authoring process. A practitioner will initiate the double story by expanding on this understanding and using basic maps of externalizing and positional mapping. In addition, dipping into the landscape of action by asking for examples is helpful. How much is valued and treasured reveals nuances to explore.

Next, the facilitator turns the re-authoring around by asking how that significant person would speak about the storyteller. *What did you contribute to this person's life?* Switching the question around makes the storyteller move into the landscape of identity. Honoring a significant person or organization brings new and fresh realizations that may be useful in re-creating a new identity or re-shaping the original identity.

Through the practice of opening space and stepping into the idea of re-authoring maps, you begin a major shift in the understanding of how stories shape identity and are fluid and adaptable. Using a re-authoring map gives the client a new path to developing a new belief about their identity, stepping into a new narrative where values, actions, and attitudes shape a richer self-identity. The following sections present some narrative re-authoring questions to keep in mind.

Re-Authoring Maps – Narrative questions about relationships begin by orienting the storyteller, inviting them to think about three different relationships they have experienced:

   a. An identity from their past the client has always known was a significant person in their life

b. A group, ideology, or movement that they have felt very much a part of (e.g., the anti-war movement, a church, a sports team)
c. A problem that changed their relationship

As a facilitator, you then begin to ask questions of the first identity as seen in the sample here:

Sample Questions for Relationship #1

1. Can you tell me a bit about your relationship with this person?
2. What did this person most appreciate about you?
3. If you saw yourself through this person's eyes, how would you describe yourself?
4. What were you in touch with about yourself when you were with this person?
5. What does "being" this way (the way they have described in the above question) contribute to this person's life?
6. How would you describe your identity in this relationship?

Sample Questions for Relationship #2

1. Can you tell me about your participation in this group or movement?
2. If you actively chose this group or movement, what about it attracted you?
3. With what were you affiliating in joining this group or movement?
4. What can you see in yourself in reviewing your participation?
5. What did you contribute to this group or movement?
6. If you could interview other members, what might they tell me about you?

The Art of Narrative

7. What was it like having a sense that someone saw you in this way?
8. How (these could be very small ways) was this group or local version of the movement different with your participation?
9. Were there times in relation to this group or movement when you felt like you were participating in something larger than yourself? What was that like?
10. How would you describe your identity in this relationship?

Sample Questions for Relationship #3

1. Can you tell me about this problem as you used to experience it? What were some of this problem's effects back then?
2. What has changed about your relationship with this problem? How did that change come about? Were other people important in facilitating this change?
3. Now that you have changed your relationship with the problem, what is different about your life?
4. What do you know now about yourself that you didn't know when the problem obscured your view?
5. How does your new relationship with this problem affect your contributions in the world?
6. If the problem could speak, what would it most respect about you as a "worthy adversary?"
7. How did changing your relationship with the problem change your identity?
8. How would you name or describe your identity in this new relationship with the problem?

Connecting The Three Relationships

Now, ask your client to imagine, one at a time, seeing him or herself in each of the identities discussed in the example (or, if they already see themselves in an identity, how would they see it more fully). Here are some sample questions for this part:

1. Is each of these different than your usual view? How?
2. Do you like seeing yourself in each of these ways? Why?
3. What difference would it make in your life and ongoing affiliations to keep each of these views alive?
4. What difference would it make to the communities in which you participate if you more fully embody these in your day-to-day life?

Conclusion

Conclude this round by having a conversation about the process, the differences in the three views, and whether there is a place (or could be a place) in your client's life for all of them.

Hopefully, this was an enjoyable exploration of re-authoring another person's story. Narrative process calls this a thickening of a single story which leads from a single story to a double story. The series of questions opens many interesting avenues for clients seeking depth of understanding and insight into their lives. Sharing stories promotes insight and awareness, challenging our daily experiences and beliefs in a supportive way that allows for change. This ripple effect after the sharing embraces how our human emotional brain assimilates and accommodates new knowledge and invites new beginnings.

In conclusion, here are three things to keep in mind:

- Do not be afraid to adjust questions to make sense of them for your client. For example, the question "With what were you

affiliating in joining this group or movement?" may not make sense to your client. You could ask instead: "What were the values you aligned yourself to when participating in the group?"
- Always remember to continually summarize and affirm your client's responses.
- Provide overviews wherever possible. Clients love the reminder.

Enjoy the process of re-authoring someone else's story.

Narrative Question for Personal Growth:
Think about the "Child" (playful and responsive) in you.
- What is it that this child encourages you to do or say that you avoid?

CHAPTER 11
Re-Membering Conversations

The term "re-membering practices" was first used by Barbara Meyerhof (1978). Michael White began to use it in 1997 to think of inviting others into narrative conversations without the "others" being present. In fact, White often referred to the idea of having a "club" where a storyteller can connect with someone in their past and acknowledge a new and fresh membership with that person. Some people are invited, and others are not.

As we move into thickening our stories, we will bring others into our conversation by choice. Re-membering maps allow storytellers to intentionally choose people who have provided worthiness in their life. Think of a club where you have the right to gather members to be part of your life membership. It raises and elevates the contributions they have made in your life. The prefix re- is specific to narrative work. It is about being reminded and recollecting the value others have made. The narrative questions are about others, past, present, and future, who have impacted or supported our lives. For many storytellers, "re-membering" raises awareness of certain people who have a strong influence in their lives but may or may not remain toxic. Toxic members may be downsized, and non-toxic members may be honored to a higher status because they contribute worthiness to your life.

Another major contribution when using re-membering questions is that we are inviting a community to challenge our western idea of individualism. If we consider the African idea of "Ubuntu," we are a collective entity, not isolated. We shape each other by the deeds and words we use. Holding the value of others in your work and identity is humbling and gracious.

Often, the practitioner keeps zigzagging between the landscape of action/events and the landscape of identity. Practitioners intentionally ask questions of positive people, or organizations/clubs, that contributed to their values or choices in life. They also explore when the storyteller experienced a problem and successfully solved it.

Practitioners may explore an alternative viewpoint by asking:

- Who would know about this?
- Who else would know that this person had this impact on you?
- Who would be least surprised to hear this about you?

Remember to remain curious. Flipping the perspective from the storyteller to how another person's perspective allows the storyteller a lens from which to honor how others value them. In addition, it accesses knowledge that is deeply hidden in the subconscious. Scaffolding through the storyteller's values, desires, principles, and beliefs using other people in the storyteller's context enriches those who may have influenced the choices the storyteller made and may wish to make in the future.

A re-membering conversation may include questions such as:

- Could you think of a value or attribute you exhibit in your work that makes you proud?
- How important is that to you? Why?
- Tell me more about how that fits with some of the other commitments you have made in your life.
- Who in your life would be least surprised about this commitment you have made in your life?
- Tell me a little more about this person. When did they come into your life? What were some of the things they valued?
- What might this person have noticed about you that spoke to your commitment?
- How would this person view your commitment today? Why?

- If you were to see yourself through this person's eyes, what would you most appreciate about yourself? What difference would that make to how you see your future work?

Facilitators may link insights from re-membering practices with people, organizations, and solutions to secure a new understanding with the storyteller. Stay curious, track impact, and once you have the connections, ask yourself if this works for the storyteller.

Narrative Question for Personal Growth:
Think about someone who impacted you significantly somewhere in your life.

- What would this person say to you today?

CHAPTER 12
Scaffolding Conversations

Scaffolding narrative conversations are primarily used for professionals seeking more depth and connection within the experiences in their lives. Awareness and empowerment are present in those seeking a scaffolding conversation. Making meaning out of the relationships that have impacted life invites different wisdom into one's life. Facilitators ask the storyteller to identify three areas for discussion: (a) a personally significant relationship with someone, (b) an organization or group the person experienced a sense of community with, and (c) a problem that they resolved successfully.

If witnesses are present, the role of the witness honors the identities only at the end of the four phases of the conversation. Witnesses remember to focus on any of the following four aspects of the story:

- **Identify expressions**
  "I noticed the repeated use of words like resourcefulness and awareness as you described yourself. At what age did you recognize these qualities?"

- **Describe images**
  "The image you used of a tree spoke volumes in how the advocacy work you did brought about changes for others."

- **Embody responses**
  "I got in touch with your ability to enjoy each experience as it arrived."

- **Acknowledge where the story transported you**
  "When you spoke of how your mother protected you from physical abuse, it helped me understand why your commitment to children is so evident in your current work."

The connecting of the three stories requires the facilitator and/or witnesses to make notes of phrases and identities that are mentioned. This allows the summary at the end to be more meaningful. The questions asked contain skills already covered in previous chapters. These questions may be used to guide you. Enjoy the experience of thickening someone's story in this way.

Re-authoring conversations use scaffolding practices that a facilitator needs to keep in mind. They range from intentions and purposes to values and beliefs, to hopes and dreams, and finally to principles and commitment. The explanation below provides an example.

Scaffolding questions introduce the facilitator to a series of developments that increase the thickening of a story. A story that is chosen does not have to be one of adversity or a problem. It could be something happy, recent, or an example from work. Facilitators may move from meaning to deeper connections between the event and the person's life. The scaffolding map provides an accessible road to deeper conversations where meaning-making happens.

1. **Low-Level Distancing Questions - Meaning-making.**
   What name would you give to this experience? Does it mean anything to you?

2. **Medium-Level Distancing Questions - Bringing things into a relationship, making connections between events.**
   How does this fit with your life right now? What does this motivate you to look at?

3. **Lateral.**
   Was anyone else surprised to see you doing these things? Why do you think that is?

4. **Medium to High-Level Distancing Questions - Reflection on identity.**
   What did this event tell you about your values?

OR use any of the scaffolding aspects linked to identity as seen below:
* **Intention/Purpose**
* **Values/Beliefs**
* **Hopes/Dreams**
* **Principles**
* **Commitments**

5. **High-Level Distancing Questions - Transport and proposals for steps to take.**
As you are thinking about these values or commitments, where has this taken you in terms of where you want to be or go?

Scaffolding Questions
Scaffolding Maps
Scaffolding Conversation 1: Exploring the Impact of Historical Trauma

1. Choose from the dimensions of nationality, ethnicity, or religion. What is your large group identity and trauma?
2. What does this mean to you presently?
3. How has the knowledge of the identity/trauma been passed on to you?
4. How might that get passed on to others? Give examples. What aspects of it are you aware of? What ways might you pass it on of which you are unaware?
5. What effects are there of passing on the large group's chosen identity/trauma?
6. What are the values you hold essential in your life?
7. What would you wish to do about passing on the historical identity/trauma?
8. What kind of support could you enlist to accomplish this?

Chapter 12

Scaffolding Conversation 2: Exploring the Journey Toward Wisdom

1. What experiences have you had that propelled you in doing what you are currently doing?
2. Have you shared any of these developments with anyone in your life?
3. If so, who has been particularly receptive to learning about these "wise" ways?
4. If not, who might benefit or be supportive of learning this?
5. If you imagine that developing these strengths and wise ways is taking you on a journey, what kind of journey would you imagine it to be?
6. What and who stands to benefit from where you could take your wisdom and knowledge?
7. If you were to celebrate your journey, what legacy might you wish to leave behind?

Adapted from Weingarten, K. (2003), The Witnessing Project (www.WitnessingProject.org).

These conversations may take place over a series of sessions if you wish to allow time in between. Again, making sound notes not to lose the crux of the identities is important. Concluding the conversation using the meta-discussion of the process promotes solidifying nuggets of wisdom that may be worth inviting more intentionally into daily living. When we are younger, unique opportunities are often glanced over like a sinking ship. Re-authoring by salvaging parts of these younger memories can reconnect with the present in a way that is meaningful. Re-authoring conversations helps us honor these experiences in a positive tribute and as a contribution to one's journey of self-discovery.

Narrative Question for Personal Growth:

- Is there a bad habit you wish to challenge yourself in?

CHAPTER 13
Compassionate Witnessing

Compassionate witnessing may happen personally or in a structured approach in training. An example of a personal compassionate witnessing would be any harmful interaction where your affective questions or statements act as a catalyst for reflection by the other. For example, Mary, a mother of a screaming toddler waiting her turn at the checkout counter, is berated by a man standing in line, saying, *"You are a useless mother if you cannot keep your child in check!"* The cashier, hearing this, would compassionately say, *"I am saddened by what that gentleman said. Is there anything I can do to help you right now?"*

Often within a personal capacity, we forget how powerful compassionate witnessing can be. Compassionate witnessing can also be experienced in a group. Teaching students and others to be present with someone else's pain or suffering is hard but requires structure and a way to practice the 5 Cs we have addressed earlier.

Compassionate witnessing introduces a thickening of a narrative story by inviting witnesses to a circle in which listening to someone sharing an experience requires the presence of *now*. The incidents or events shared may or may not have been shared. The significance of the event lies in the memory of the impact of the event or incident. In formal compassionate witnessing, four circles allow the limbic system within each person to witness, share, allow impact, and debrief the incident. Individuals will choose an incident that has either a positive or a negative effect on them, giving the witness time to hear and gain a deeper awareness to honor the storyteller.

Weingarten demonstrated in her book, *Common Shock* (2003), that there are daily activities we often dismiss as incidental yet impact how we are in the world. The act of being intentional is critical when

wishing to be a compassionate witness. Three key elements exist when we intentionally witness someone else's story:
1. Selecting a focus for the story
2. Responding carefully and thoughtfully
3. Creating a bridge between us and others

In this process, oxytocin is generated in the limbic system of both the storyteller and witnesses, giving a warm and connected feeling of community.

A powerful aspect of these types of processes is that of acknowledgment. The storyteller and witness employ close listening, reflection, and exploration of resonance. Another important aspect that connects both is the guidance for witnesses to refrain from making judgments, giving advice, making conclusions, "getting autobiographical," or sharing too much of one's own story (White, 2006). Also, an attitude of curiosity and wonder is at the heart of both experiences.

Compassionate witnessing is characterized by curiosity and vulnerability. Vulnerability occurs when the storyteller shares an experience that impacted them in some way. The witnesses and facilitator remain curious and never give advice. The moment you wish to give advice, you should turn it into a question. Since compassionate witnessing comes from Family Therapy, we do not speak of the victim or offender as we would within the criminal justice community when addressing individuals. Instead, we speak of witnesses and storytellers.

Weingarten (2003) shared that, at different times in our lives, we may be witnesses, facilitators, and storytellers in varying degrees to our own story. As we take on these different roles, we gain insight into the same story from another vantage point. White referred to this as the thickening of the story. Choosing witnesses for a session requires that we guide our witnesses in nurturing strengths and giving genuine responses. The following guide listed here is used to assist those who participate in a compassionate witnessing process.

Defining a compassionate witness is essential as well as providing examples of what constitutes a healthy, compassionate witnessing process (Weingarten, 2003).

A compassionate witness is aware and takes action in relation to what he/she witnesses for the purpose of transforming and not exacerbating violence and violation.

Elements of compassionate witnessing:

Re-membering

Listening (non-judgmental and accepting)

When witnessing appropriately, you should:

- Be fully present (even if the connection is brief).
- Listen deeply without preconceptions.
- Ask questions that serve the speaker.
- Recognize what is implicit but not articulated in what is spoken.
- Reflecting back to the speaker what you heard.

Avoid these things that do not serve listening:

- Interrupting
- Interrogating
- Making judgments or pronouncements
- Offering advice or conclusions
- Minimizing
- Denying the veracity of the speaker's account
- Sharing one's own problems

When responding to your clients, remember the 5 Cs (see page 50), and also keep these restorative questions in mind to use when appropriate. Restorative Questions 1 can be used when challenging behaviors cause harm to others, and Restorative Questions 2 are asked of those experiencing harm.

Restorative Questions 1 (To respond to challenging behavior.)
- What happened?
- What were you thinking of at the time?
- What have you thought about since?
- Who has been affected by what you have done? In what way?
- What do you think you need to do to make things right?

Restorative Questions 2 (To help those harmed by other actions)
- What did you think when you realized what had happened?
- What impact has this incident had on you and others?
- What has been the hardest thing for you?
- What do you think needs to happen to make things right?

Process 1 is described in detail here. The four-circle process is a format for training that I use regularly, but if facilitators have no one else to call on, they must remember to change their role from a facilitator to a witness every now and then. It requires summarizing what was heard and being curious. This process allows one to move easily from the landscape of events to the landscape of identity.

Process 1: Compassionate Witnessing

The group is asked to appoint a timekeeper for themselves. Each session will require 90 minutes. The process of compassionate witnessing will contain four circles:

1. Dialogue between facilitator and person (sharing common shock experience)
   (Time: 8 - 15 minutes)

2. Outside witnesses having a conversation about what they heard
   (Time: 8 - 15 minutes)

3. Dialogue between the facilitator & person about the outsider's comments
   (Time: 8 -15 minutes)

4. Meta-conversation with all participants
   (Time: 8 -15 minutes)

Circle 1 (Dialogue)

- Facilitator to ask the narrative map questions that are appropriate for the session.
- Remember to ask extended questions in between (e.g., how, what, whose, why).
- Remain neutral and curious.

Circle 2 (Outside witnesses)

- This must flow like a conversation between the participants.
- No advice must be given.
- The storyteller listens in silence and can reflect later.
- Outside witnesses must respond to words and phrases the person has used.
- Take note of the responses you have to the issues.
- Ask questions of the person that can be answered later.
- Be respectful of the person's story.
- If you do ask another outside witnessing person how they handled a similar situation, remember to place it back with the identified person's story.

Circle 3 (Dialogue)

The facilitator asks the person questions about what they just heard:

- What did you connect with?
- Why?
- What did you think when so and so said this?
- Where is this taking you now?

Circle 4 (All participants)

- What was it like for you to tell your story?
- How did you feel as the facilitator?

- Open the discussion to the group where you are free to ask the facilitator why they were asked certain questions.
- Comment on where you felt a shift happen in the compassionate process.
- What was it that made the shift?

Scaffolding is where witnesses learn the art of listening to words and recognizing how they resonate with you. Scaffolding allows witnesses to respond naturally to ways in which a word used or repeated impacts the storyteller. The Relational Care Ladder (Rundell, 2017) supports the scaffolding process from structure to nurture and finally to engagement (see Diagram 3).

When facilitators wish to train witnesses, they may start by getting a group comfortable with silent circles before introducing them to affirmation circles. This progression allows participants to learn the first two rungs of the Relational Care Ladder. Next, participants can experience listening circles using the structure and nurture rungs. The structure allows them to feel comfortable and acknowledge self-worth as an explicit norm. Compassionate witnessing circles invite three rungs of the ladder (i.e., structure, nurture, and engagement). One person's story is shared with vulnerability and curiosity and can be truly sacred.

* Silent circles provide a structure that communicates safety while maintaining silence as participants arrange objects in the center space. Meditation circles come to mind. Activities that take place in silent circles promote keen observation for participants.

* Listening circles allow the safety and awareness of the impact of issues to be heard (i.e., structure and nurture).

* Compassionate witnessing circles use the first three rungs of the Relational Care Ladder, where the client's needs of safety, awareness, and feelings are explored.

Process 2: Listening Circles

What listening circles are NOT
- Dialogue
- Discussion
- Facilitators giving advice
- Judgment on how others have been impacted
- A process to fix the problem

Our Agreement for small group gatherings
1. I recognize the facilitator as the moderator.
2. I will answer only the questions that are asked.
3. I will speak when holding the "Talking Piece."
4. I will not comment on what others have said.
5. I can pass if I do not wish to share.
6. I will be respectful at all times.

Process
- Open with a check-in: a fun fact.
- Read through the agreement your group has approved.
- Choose the topic for the three questions.
- No more than five in a group.
- Meta-discussion closure after the small group go-around: "What words or phrases stood out for you as you listened?"
- Close with "What did you learn, realize, or what surprised you during the listening circle?"

Listening Circle (each person is limited to a maximum of 2 minutes each time.)
- **First Question:**
  What impact does _____ have on your life?

- **Second Question:**
  What has been most difficult for you talking about this?
- **Third Question:**
  What one support would you wish to put in place for yourself?
- **Meta-discussion:**
  What word or phrases did you hear in our listening circle?

This chapter introduced compassionate witnessing as a process that may thicken a client's story. Allowing the scaffolding process addresses the needs of the individual within the circle in a systemic way and invites a richer experience of re-membership and re-authoring, honoring our daily lives. One tip in introducing compassionate witnessing is to begin with silent circles and then move to affirmation circles. The skills learned prepare witnesses to experience the power of listening circles and compassionate witnessing circles. Enjoy using the processes identified in the appendices. Find ways to introduce different aspects of scaffolding into your work and family life.

Narrative Question for Personal Growth:
- When has someone else's non-verbal role modeling influenced you? What changes did you bring into your life because of that?

CHAPTER 14
Documentation, Letter Writing, Arts, and Nature

The beauty of having a narrative conversation is the ability to establish a dominant story, then move away into a preferred reality, allowing space for discovery with no restrictions. Art, music, nature, letter writing, the creation of documents, and many other manifestations are concrete ways of engaging the right brain in an exploration of a different kind. Providing concrete experiences allows time for the neural pathways to feel and reflect on an earlier, buried commitment to a sense of purpose.

Weingarten (2003) discussed the four universal knowledges that assist healing: ceremony and ritual, community, art, and nature. Within narrative inquiry, we deepen the stories through our connections with these four universal knowledges. The global experience of the COVID-19 pandemic has allowed recognition and awareness of how essential universal knowledge is to human development. Rituals and ceremonies enable structures to be put into place that provide feelings of security and safety. Think of the number of deaths experienced during COVID-19 in which family members could not visit their dying loved ones. Many were bereft without closure due to their inability to provide a ritual of closure through a funeral or memorial service. Honoring a loved one's life is a closing ritual, and communities bring together the warm feelings that generate oxytocin. A hug or the touch of a gentle hand speaks volumes in making the human connection.

Identifying different forms of art ranges from drawing, letter writing, journaling, storytelling, making puppets, sewing, knitting, music, poetry, sculpting, and many other forms. The artmaking itself heals because it promotes focus and space in which time stops for the healing. Practicing some form of art can be compared to meditation because it frees the neural pathways to flow without inhibitions. Science has shown amazing changes to the brain if done regularly. Exploring alternative stories in our lives is invigorating and allows creative ideas to emerge. Preferred stories are all about an invitation to explore with no risk to one's identity.

All art forms may enrich conversations by using the process with the client to produce a climate of mutuality and reciprocity. Unique and sparkling moments arise through the creativity of working on a piece of art. The essential reason art is so powerful is that the right brain engages, allowing a different perspective to be accessed. The left brain is sequential, whereas the right brain is holistic and sees an overview.

Nature thickens a story in a unique way. Beta and theta waves are emitted when walking through a forest or on the beach. This is critical in refreshing the flow of energy through the body. Walks and hikes in nature, playing games outside, skiing, and snowboarding all have the same impact. Movement and breathing create new levels of restoration. Going on a hike or a nature trail may reveal curiosity and discussion that opens an alternative reality. Narrative inquiry is not restricted to the four walls of an office or room. The invitation to have coffee or a picnic can be used to reconnect with the client.

Therapeutic documents may range from a SWOT analysis (Strengths, Weaknesses, Opportunities, and Threats), writing of dreams, writing down a mantra as a reminder for daily living, or acknowledging of self or a behavior pattern you wish to embrace. One document I have used with clients that I find valuable is four pieces of paper; each piece of paper is labeled as follows:

1. Where are you now?
2. Where do you want to be in the future?
3. What are the gaps?
4. What steps do you need to take to meet the gaps?

Each document (1 to 4) serves as a guide for a client to uncover the alternative story.

Therapeutic letters invite the reflection of attributes that need to be recalled. Through continual reading, they can bring up a different sense of self-worth that may get lost in the dominant story. A common practice is to provide a sandwich in a letter: Offer an affirmation of worth with assets that are apparent then insert a challenge the client chooses. Close the sandwich with encouragement and belief in the client.

Using objects and toys can remind one of a unique moment or gratitude that needs to be invited into daily living. White asked clients to choose an object in his room that would and could act as a reminder of the commitment made.

The richness of bringing in documentation, letters, art, or nature invites facilitators to be open to exploring the client's interests and wishes. Using one modality is sufficient for delving into a passion; however, consistency, predictability, and unconditional regard must be present throughout. Being in connection with other human beings while engaging in any art form creates a higher level of belonging and intention.

"Deep listening is the kind of listening that can help relieve the suffering of another person. You can call it compassionate listening. You listen with only one purpose: to help him or her to empty his heart...

Because you know that listening like that, you give that person a chance to suffer less. If you want to help him to correct his perception, you wait for another time...You just listen with compassion and help him to suffer less. One hour like that can bring transformation and healing." (Thich Nhat Hanh)

Narrative Question for Personal Growth:
Think about an animal, an object, or a phrase that describes you. Spend some time drawing or writing a letter to that animal, object, or phrase.

- What did you learn, realize, or what surprised you?

CHAPTER 15
Co-vision and Co-research

Defining Co-vision

Community work and supervision have a history of power structures and struggles. Co-vision is a post-modern process that challenges the notion of power, language usage, self, and relational identity (Rundell, 2001). It is a fluid and dynamic process dependent on the reflective-practitioner context and the group's intent. Co-vision is a term used as an alternative to supervision.

One key feature that professionals often suffer from is empathic stress. *What is an empathic stress reaction?* An empathetic stress reaction is a term that encompasses two types of persistent common shock that do not get better with time. Even the act of compassionate witnessing is not enough to help those suffering from empathic stress reactions. Empathic stress reactions are common in professionals whose jobs require frequent witnessing of traumatic events, whether first-hand viewing of abuse, violence, or other acts of violation or working closely with those who have had first-hand experience with such acts.

Individuals in these types of professions (including teachers, clergy, law enforcement officers, journalists, and counselors) may be more susceptible to empathic stress reactions for several reasons, including (a) their personal nature, which brought them to the compassionate work in the first place, (b) the guilt that may be felt about not being able to do more, and (c) the simple fact that they are humans. Weingarten (2003) stated, "No amount of training for the performance of their duties ... changes the fact that these professionals do their jobs inside bodies that work the same way in their professional lives" (p. 100).

Two specific types of empathic stress reactions are burnout and secondary traumatic stress. Burnout occurs when individuals feel they can no longer be successful in their jobs due to the pressures of the work. As Weingarten stated, "on the job, stresses gradually mount so that the person feels less and less able to accomplish the goals for which [they] entered the profession. Often there are institutional or structural barriers that interfere with the person's ability to work effectively" (p. 101). While burnout occurs as a result of the overall impact of witnessing on the job, secondary traumatic stress relates to the impact of witnessing on an individual who has experienced specific harm or witnessed first-hand harmful experiences on the job. Secondary traumatic stress is a powerful response, the symptoms of which "may be profoundly disturbing to a professional who subscribes to the belief that his training renders him invulnerable to distress" (Weingarten, 2003, p. 102). Secondary traumatic stress symptoms range from psychological (i.e., distressing emotions, sadness, rage, fear, horror, emotional numbness), physical (i.e., rapid heartbeat, sweating, heightened vigilance, difficulty concentrating, insomnia), and behavioral (i.e., difficulty maintaining schedule, drug and alcohol abuse, ignoring self-care).

The process for co-vision follows the compassionate witnessing format identified in Weingarten (2003). Co-vision sessions may use any type of circle format the group decides on when they gather. The options are:

1. Listening Circles (see Process 2, Chapter 13)
2. Compassionate Witnessing Circles (see Process 1, Chapter 13)
3. Solution-Focused Circles

These three types of circles have different formats as noted in Chapter 13. Each process addresses a different need on the Relational Care Ladder (see Diagram 3). The solution-focused circle requires that a facilitator give a person seeking a solution five minutes to explain the issue then witnesses spend 5-10 minutes brainstorming gifts that may address the problem. The person requesting help then chooses one or two ideas. No names are used, which acknowledges only the ideas generated. The awareness of alternatives may generate further ripple effects. The format may be used in schools and organizations with any sort of content. Using this format in different restorative practice settings is often referred to as professional learning groups (Sheety & Rundell, 2012).

Awareness is not a single act but a continuous action; it is a verb. In awareness, the intentionality of how we listen becomes important. Sharing openly with empathy, safety, and awareness is key.

Defining Co-Research

Michael White (2007) used the term "co-researcher" to describe how "I-would-be-in-the-world" as an invitation to be in relation to others in a genuine and equal way. How we document the interaction introduces a qualitative analysis of ground theory research. Using qualitative constructs to study and analyze human connections within relationships and communities has a dynamic synergy.

An Example of Co-Research

In our co-vision groups, one witness is chosen to be the poetic witness and record phrases that the storyteller shares. At the end of the compassionate witnessing, the poetic witness asks to share phrases spoken during the storytelling in the form of a poem. These poems may be collected, shared, edited, and published as a book. Collaborative work within a community benefits the participants and enhances growth and well-being.

Narrative Question for Personal Growth:
Inquiry and mindfulness are the same. They each come from different

ends of a continuum. Asking questions and paying attention to the *now* does not require answers.

- What would happen if you practiced the three basic principles: *Dignity, No Harm,* and *Acceptance*? Test yourself and find out.

CHAPTER 16
Definitional Ceremonies, Rituals, and Ceremonies

Think of the number of rituals we must mark as significant events in our lives. Here are just a few: wedding ceremonies, burial services, memorial services, baptisms, bar mitzvahs, bas mitzvahs, and graduation ceremonies. Christian, Jewish, and Muslim celebrations have intentional rituals to memorialize special days, but what is the meaning of having such celebrations or rituals? The purpose is to honor a special event or occasion in life or the history of an individual or a group. Rituals and celebrations are structures that create a safe space to acknowledge awareness and nurture loyalty.

Definitional ceremonies, as introduced by Michael White, are a way to invite a significant person into a client's life to hear and honor the changes made from a dominant story to an alternative story or choice. For example, Alcoholics Anonymous has rituals in which individuals use witnesses to hold themselves accountable for their commitments to sobriety. Similarly, definitional ceremonies hold a witness's presence as a support to a client's efforts to change their reality. When working with your client, asking who to invite as a witness is important. Accept any response, as the client should be able to express which friends or family might be comfortable or uncomfortable to include.

Another option to consider is having a compassionate witness unknown to the client. The unknown witness must be skilled in encouragement and compassion. In addition, the unknown witness may highlight and honor the storyteller with integrity and wisdom that could surprise the storyteller.

Reflecting the storyteller's own words back to them is also an option. Gathering some of the words and phrases your client has spoken over the weeks and creating free verse or prose may be a useful way of witnessing back to your client. Often, the most profound statements your storyteller shares are lost. This is one way of honoring them. Here is an example of a poem constructed after listening to a storyteller:

Victim to Victor

There is a difference between Victim and Victor.
I did not know.
I never realized I experienced trauma.
My faith helped straighten me out.

Experiencing common shock.
Talking to my brothers
Creating space to talk
Sharing my story.

I didn't pause,
I had to protect my brother and mom.
I had no other choice but to
make sure they were okay.

When my mom left us,
my grandma became my rock.
She looked after us,
but there was no food.

When I was kidnapped from her,
I would write five-page love letters to her.
Her words helped me overcome.
"Remember, you are God's children."

I love my family,
but I have to protect myself.
As part of the family,
you have to accept shame.

I need to grieve and bury my Dad.
I have no memory of Grade 8.
Dad, I love you.
I forgive you.

Rituals and ceremonies of closure are worth considering at this stage of the therapeutic relationship. Bedtime and mealtime rituals are appropriate ways to establish safety. Regular patterns within families, the classroom, and businesses allow individuals to have an expectancy that brings a sense of community. When closing with your client, this may be setting a time and place to meet once every few weeks for a cup of coffee and check-in or making a regular schedule for visits. This extends the therapeutic alliance to a continual support system that nurtures and cares. Definitional ceremonies are one way of closing with a therapeutic alliance while allowing space for a continuation of care. Encouraging other rituals and ceremonies are sound ways to bring safety into relationships for moments of awareness and community stability.

Narrative Question for Personal Growth:
A rock is a symbol for grounding.

- How do you use your rock when you get triggered by a bad, sad, mad, or glad thought or event in your day?

CHAPTER 17
Ethics

"Practicing an art, no matter how well or badly, is a way to make your soul grow. Sing in the shower. Dance to the radio. Tell stories. Write a poem to a friend, even a lousy poem. Do it as well as you possibly can. You will get an enormous reward. You will have created something." (Kurt Vonnegut)

As narrative facilitators, we must pay close attention to the ethical stance of working within a post-modern framework. "In a post-modern world, ethics focus on particular people in particular experiences, and there is considerable skepticism about the applicability of any kind of sweeping, universal, one-size-fits-all truth claims" (Freedman & Combs, 1996, p. 265). One of the most important ways we can do this is to consider how particular practices affect people in local cultures. As White and Epson demonstrated, holding a set of questions to guide the narrative relationship can be very useful. The questions used reflect narrative ethics. Four key questions are asked when using narrative inquiry (Freedman & Combs, 1996):

- Question the **power dynamic** in the process.
  Ask yourself, "Do the questions invite the storytellers to be the experts in their life?"
- Are the questions **separating the deed from the doer**?
  Ask yourself, "Do questions open spaces that allow a deeper exploration of the middle of the story?"

- Do you remain **intentionally curious** and connected?
  Are you "being" in relationship with the storyteller and not making assumptions? Freedman and Combs (1996) stated, "We seek to join them in their experience of the world" (p. 277). To do this, it is important to listen genuinely and value what is being shared.

- Do you remain **with** the storyteller and allow growth through an emotional connection of empathy and compassion?

Ethical issues in any narrative process require the facilitator's awareness of the context of the client's intent.

Post-modern ethics "is expressed, not as rules or formulas, but rather as questions that invite *practitioners* to examine their own awareness in terms of the relationships and practices that bring forth the thickening of a story" (Freedman & Combs, 1996, p. 265). The idea is to keep the focus on people and relationships and the effects of our practices.

Diagram 7 is a cross-shaped diagram that explains Karl Tomm's set of ethical postures. The vertical access provides the option to decrease options, using lineal assumptions; the alternative is to increase options for thickening a story by using circular assumptions. The latter option leads to changes in the emotional brain. The horizontal access uses knowledge to orientate intentions with selective exposure to information; whereas the opposite is to be transparent, sharing knowledge to influence intention. Facilitators are encouraged to strive to work with circular assumptions while empowering with a shared knowledge. Discretion in sharing information needs to be a continual ethical awareness.

Diagram 7: Tomm's Ethical Grid

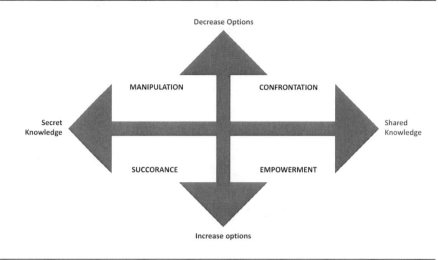

Tomm, K. (1988).

Tomm created four guiding principles to empower himself and others. These principles are active (verb) words that hold within them the implication of alive and ongoing movement between self and relationship.

1. **Grounding** - being sensitive, attending to context and conditions, listening deeply, and sharing descriptions

2. **Recursion-ing** - being mindful by listening to others listening and assuming that assumptions are being made

3. **Coherence-ing** - being congruent includes identifying inconsistencies between intent and effect and privileges in emotional dynamics to reach internal congruence

4. **Authenticating** - being honest which includes privileging direct experience over explanations and being open to seeing oneself through others' eyes

Safran and Muran (2000) stated that the "therapeutic meta-communication requires mindfulness in action. Therapists and practitioners alike need to practice these skills with great regularity. When experiencing a therapeutic impasse, mindfulness in action needs to be at the forefront. Blaming within the therapeutic alliance means that there are unconscious motivations, defenses and relational patterns that are at play. There is the likelihood that countertransference reactions will interfere with the narrative process. Countertransference disclosures play an important role in meta-communication in articulating an implicit or intuitive sense. It then makes the implicit, explicit. Once consciousness is raised, awareness to work on the issue is possible. If you do not acknowledge it, you cannot begin to work on it.

A storyteller needs to process the naming of their experiences first before they can claim it. Once ownership of a story is present, the reframing of the issue is the thickening of the story. If witnesses are called in to listen, the storyteller is ready to proclaim their perceptions and experiences to an audience. Another aspect of reclaiming allows the storyteller to use taking it back practices. These will be discussed in more detail later in this chapter.

What are the Ethical Issues We, as Narrative Practitioners, Must Pay Attention To?

Freedman and Combs (1996) encouraged an awareness of the norms of different cultures and ethnicities as well as seeing family members as ordinary people with difficult life experiences. As practitioners, we should avoid pressuring storytellers to fit into their cultural norms; this is unethical and damaging. Above all, it is disrespectful. Freedman and Combs assert that making room for marginalized voices and marginalized cultures is an essential ethical imperative in narrative inquiry. The belief is that it is "…a 'margin-in' approach to ethics - one which values the experience of people at the margins of any dominant culture or at the bottom of any culture's hierarchies and takes a strong ethical stance in favor of making space for such peoples' voices to be heard, understood, and to allow for a response."

Two of the questions used by White and Epston to guide facilitators in their ethical practice are:

1. Do questions asked lead in a generative or normative direction (e.g., propose alternative or conserve dominant social practices)?

2. Does the model require the person to enter the practitioner's "expert" knowledge, or does it require the practitioner to enter the "world" of the storyteller (Freedman & Combs, 1996)?

Maturana defines violence as "any imposition of one's will upon another" and love as "opening space for the existence of the other" (cited in Freedman & Combs, p. 271). On the issue of violence, White and Tomms are drawn to loving care and repelled by violence. Both narrative authors encourage assisting the storyteller in the co-creation of empowerment and discretionary options. This position gives pause in knowing and valuing willingness to asking open ended questions and never assume or judge another person's story. The concept of co-creation between the practitioners and the storyteller becomes essential when engaging in narrative conversations.

Narrative practices are borne out of respect for all humans. Through the practice of listening intentionally, respect and nonjudgment provide the structure and nurturing essential for compassionate spaces. Narrative practitioners do not prescribe actions that will fix a problem. Rather, it is about making space for possible unique outcomes through conversations about values and commitments the storyteller desires for themselves.

Why is "Taking It Back" an Important Concept for Narrative Practitioners?

Taking it back is very important; it places the alternative or preferred story into an action focus. When you have spent so much time in the process of identifying unique outcomes, re-membering, and re-authoring, you need to share this knowledge with others. The storyteller is accountable for sharing the benefits of having been listened to and may wish to share it with anyone they choose. The take it back step involves looking at the storyteller's commitments to self and others and how they want to live their life. Allowing the knowledge of the connections to form part of their ongoing community allows the support needed to continue with awareness.

The acknowledgment of remembering and communicating is an important part of how Michael White encouraged a ripple effect. For example, Michael White would ask a storyteller at the end of a conversation if there was an object in his room that the storyteller wanted to take to remind them of what they discussed. Also, he would remind the storyteller of the awareness they accomplished. Then, he would have them take an object home. The hope was for the storyteller to share their knowledge with someone else.

The takeaway could be a letter written to affirm the storyteller's commitment to themselves and to read whenever they experience vulnerability. An example of this was Julius, who experienced voices. Julius entered an elevator with several people, and the voices began to bother him. As the voices grew louder, he pulled out the letter he had written when with his facilitator and read it aloud. At the next stop, everyone got out except for a young woman. She addressed him by saying, "Please, could you share that letter with me. I have a brother who experiences exactly what you have. The contents of your letter would help him." This example demonstrates the taking it back practice.

Narrative ethics solely focuses on the relationship. Relational alliances continually change; therefore, checking in and adjusting expectations and assumptions strengthens the alliance.

The art of narrative is an ancient practice of storytelling. It reminds us to use whatever comes up and wherever we find ourselves, as an occasion for inquiry, for opening, and for growing in dignity, not causing harm, and in acceptance.

Chapter 17

Many times, we feel unheard or invisible in life. Our own stories are buried treasures waiting to be given away as gifts for those willing to listen.

> *Learning to facilitate a lifeline through the centuries is truly an art.*
> *Many of us hold our stories inside.*
> *We may think they are not important.*
> *We may feel there is no one who listens.*
> *We may not be aware that they are even there.*

But as the great Irish poet David Whyte wrote:

> *"To be human is to become visible while carrying what is hidden as a gift to others."*

Narrative Question for Personal Growth:

- When we are *Whole*, we are *One* with the Universe. What brings *Wholeness* and *Purpose* to your daily life?

Glossary of Narrative Terms

Compassionate witnessing circles:

A process of listening to someone's story with a group of witnesses. It provides structure and a way to embody the responses of the storyteller that are non-judgmental and empathetic. Outside witnesses are key to bringing new insights.

Co-research:

Term used by Michael White (2007) to describe the qualitative process of equalizing the relationship between the professional and client that creates the dynamic synergy of shared participation.

Co-vision:

A compassionate witnessing process where a group of colleagues may share experiences. Co-vision is an alternative to supervision and has no hierarchy involved.

Cybernetics:

Communication and connection within the nervous system and brain. This science studies the relation of these systems within the body.

Definitional ceremonies/outside witnesses:

In narrative practice, significant others are often invited to stand as "outsider witnesses" to the person's preferred developments. In response to the person's "telling" of these developments, the witnesses are invited, in a "re-telling" process, to reflect on what struck a chord for them and to connect resonant themes with their own lives. The therapist carefully structures this witnessing as a kind of ceremony, in which talk is directed towards supporting the person's agentive stories, values, behaviors, and experiences. The ceremony can facilitate the emergence of new ideas and themes for further re-authoring and re-membering conversations, but its primary purpose is to begin a process of thickening and grounding the person's preferred ways of being in communal life and spaces (for further reading, see White, 2007, Chapter 4).

Externalizing maps:
- to make external or externally manifest
- to attribute to causes outside the self: rationalize the externalized lack of ability to succeed

They refer to the conversational practice of separating the person from the problem, which is thereby externalized. In practice, this involves speaking about the problem as external to the person and as exerting influence on them (e.g., the claim "I am anorexic" might lead the therapist to ask a question(s) such as, "How does anorexia persuade you to treat your body?").

Four-circle process:

This refers to the series four distinct segments processes used in compassionate witnessing. Generally, each process follows: 1. A facilitator invites a storyteller to share an event on their mind, 2. The witnesses reflect back with compassion using care, encouragement, compassion, curiosity and connection about the story's impact, 3. The facilitator and storyteller reflect on what is heard from the witnesses, 4. The group reflects on the overall experience of the first three circles.

Landscape of identity/consciousness:

The realm of human experience in which we make meaning of the events that happen to us and develop understandings of the connections between events by reference to culturally learned discourse.

Landscape of events/action:

Landscape of action questions tie new stories about meaning and motivation to concrete actions that give context to the developing identity. An example is the question: What story can you tell me about a time when your wife's actions showed these desires?

Letter writing:

Notes express empowered perspectives that act as a reminder for someone who has been engaged in a narrative conversation. Letter writing substitutes having a witness in the conversation.

Listening circles:

A group process for a maximum of six people that invites a personal perspective on an issue. It does not involve a discussion or conversation.

Mapping:

Mapping refers to how you track someone's life story through conversations.

Through this process, people begin to see themselves as authors or at least co-authors of their own stories. As a result, they begin to move toward a greater sense of agency in their lives.

Meta-conversation:

A discussion that is based in the present. The fourth circle in compassionate witnessing is a meta-conversation about how the experience impacted each participant in the group after the storyteller and witnesses have shared.

Modernism:

Modernism refers to a global movement in society and culture that, from the early decades of the twentieth century, sought a new alignment with the experience and values of modern industrial life.

Positioning maps:

A series of narrative questions that begin with "This map provides a structure that":

- Externalizes the problem
- Acknowledges the full effects of the problem on a person's life
- Distances the person from the immediacy of the problem
- Identifies a non-problem place for the person to stand in

Post-modernism:

Post-modernism is an intellectual stance or mode of discourse defined by an attitude of skepticism toward what it considers the grand narratives of modernism and opposition to epistemic certainty and the stability of meaning. Claims of objective fact are dismissed as naive realism.

Re-authoring maps:

This conversational practice involves the development of a personal history of those behaviors, thoughts, interactions, or other experiences that run counter to or seem out of phase with problem-saturated stories and the non-preferred thoughts, behaviors, and experiences they sponsor. The therapist asks questions that move back and forth between the "landscape of action" (actual historical events and happenings in the person's life) and the "landscape of identity" (what these events suggest about the person's identity, sense of agency, ethics, values, and commitments) in an attempt to narratively thicken and foster a sense of historical depth and personal congruence in relation to preferred personal developments (see White, 2007, Chapter 2).

Re-membering maps:

The term re-membering is used because the person is seen as becoming a member of an enabling community, which may have been forgotten or not fully recognized (see White, 2007, Chapter 3).

Rituals:

Customary check-ins and check-outs, as well as other celebrations, are honored in narrative work.

Scaffolding:

Live conversations don't adapt very well to any pre-made blueprint or pre-made questionnaires; they seem to live their own lives. So, keep in mind, that it is never important for the facilitator to follow all the steps from the bottom to top around one specific theme. Scaffolding provides a basic structure in facilitating a narrative theme.

Scaffolding includes moving the live conversation with any of the parts of the scaffold. It could be about intentions/purpose; or values and beliefs; exploring hopes and dreams; or venture into principles and commitment. Questions may range from very low distancing questions to high distancing questions.

Silent circles:

Circles without words. Objects may be placed in the center of the open space and participants sequentially take turns arranging objects without speaking, handing off a talking piece when they are finished with their turn. When the facilitator ends the activity, participants can then speak about their experience during the activity.

Single story:

A single story is a one-sided point of view of something or someone. Therefore, single stories have the power to tell false or biased interpretations of the actual story.

Sparkling moments:

A moment in any problem-saturated story when the client demonstrates a surprising achievement in defeating or limiting the influence of a life problem. Such moments, which are often isolated and neglected, are the shining stars in a sky darkened by the dominance of the problem.

Taking it back:

Inviting inclusion and new associations into the conversation by re-engaging with others and sharing the benefits of narrative conversations with others who may be impacted by the knowledge.

Thickening the story/double story:

Using any of the maps that enrich new and different perspectives of a story.

Unique outcomes maps:

The unique outcomes technique involves changing one's own storyline. In narrative therapy, the client aims to construct a storyline for their experiences, which offers meaning or gives them a positive and functional identity. Narrative therapists assume that there will always be times in the person's life in which problems will be subverted or the person will be resistant to supporting narratives.

APPENDIX A
Externalizing Questions

The first basic principle in narrative is to separate the deed from the doer. When listening to your client or storyteller, the skill is to hear and identify the issue. Then use the descriptive symptom as a noun. We call this "externalizing."

For example, someone says, "I am angry with my husband for…" You may reply, "So tell me more about how Anger visits your relationship in other ways." To personify the symptom helps separate the deed from the doer.

Providing a name and meaning for the symptom is a useful way of allowing the brain time to examine issues without feeling personally attacked. Here are some examples:

X = Angry	changes to	Y = Anger
X = Anxious	changes to	Y = Anxiety
X = Competitive	changes	Y = Competition

We call this process externalizing.

X - represents any issue/symptom
Y - represents the noun form of any issue/symptom.

Externalizing Questions:

1. What made you vulnerable for the Y to most likely take over?
2. In what contexts is the Y most likely to take over?
3. What kinds of things happen that typically lead to the Y taking over?

4. What has Y gotten in to do against your better judgment?
5. What effect does the Y have on your life and relationships?
6. How has the Y led you into difficulties you are now experiencing?
7. Does the Y blind you from noticing your resources or can you see them in spite of the Y?
8. Have there been times when you have been able to get the best of the Y? Times when the Y could have taken over, but you kept it out of the picture?

APPENDIX B
Distress Scale

Stress Scale Check-In

10 – Feeling unbearably bad. Heading for an emotional breakdown. Can't talk.

9 – Feeling desperate. Unbearable. Scared. Losing control.

8 – Freaking out!! The beginning of alienation.

7 – Starting to freak out! On the edge of some definitely bad feelings. Can maintain control with difficulty.

6 – Feeling bad. Something ought to be done about the way you feel.

5 – Moderately upset, uncomfortable. Feelings are manageable with effort.

4 – Somewhat upset. You cannot ignore the thought, but you can handle it.

3 – Mildly upset. Worried or bothered to the point you notice it.

2 – A little bit upset. But you took care of yourself.

1 – No acute distress and feeling basically good.

0 – Peaceful, serene, relieved.

APPENDIX C
Exercises for Practitioners

Exercise 1: Affirmations & Reflections using Externalizing Maps

Pick a character trait, quality, or emotion that you feel you have too much of or that other people sometimes complain about in you. Make sure it is in adjective form, as a description of you, for instance, "angry," "guilty," "competitive," or "nitpicky." The trait or emotion is the "X" in the initial part of the externalizing process.

Now, as you read these questions substitute the trait or emotion "X" for a "Y" to make it a noun. This means we are taking the same quality or trait and making it into a noun. For example, if "X" was "competitive," it would now become "competition" or "angry" would become "anger." In the following questions, where we've written a "Y," fill in your noun. This is the art of externalizing.

Another way of thinking about it is to separate the deed from the doer. These questions are also scaffolded. Try it out by answering each of the following questions.

1. What made you vulnerable to the Y so that it was able to dominate your life?
2. In what contexts is the Y most likely to take over?
3. What kinds of things happen that typically lead to the Y taking over?
4. What has the Y gotten you to do that is against your better judgment?
5. What effect does the Y have on your life and relationships?

6. How has the Y led you into the difficulties you are now experiencing?

7. What has been the hardest thing for you?

8. Does the Y blind you from noticing your resources or can you see them through it?

9. Have there been times when you have been able to get the best of the Y? Times when the Y could have taken over but you kept it out of the picture?

Exercise 2: Affirmations & Reflection using Re-membering Maps

This offers reflection on successful patterns that affirm behaviors and personal qualities in order to build greater self-awareness, social awareness, and appreciation of personal dignity.

1. Describe a positive development in your work.

2. With what does this development fit?

3. Tell me a bit more about your commitment.

4. Who would be least surprised to know this about you?

5. Tell me more about this person.

6. What might this person have noticed you doing that would have suggested you held this commitment?

7. Who benefits from your latest contribution this has made in your life?

8. What would you wish to still introduce into your life that could hold the presence of that person in your work?

9. If you had to see yourself through this person's eyes, what would you most appreciate about yourself?

Exercise 3: Affirmations and Reflections using Historic Identity

This activity can provide deep, mutual appreciation for the diversity that our personal identity brings to our lives and the lives of those around us.

1. Choose from the dimensions of nationality, ethnicity, or religion. What is your large group identity and trauma?
2. What does this mean to you presently?
3. How has the knowledge of the identity/trauma been passed on to you?
4. How do you pass it on to others? Exactly? What aspects are you aware of? In what ways might you pass it on of which you are unaware?
5. What effects are there of passing on the large group's chosen identity/trauma?
6. What are the values you hold essential in your life?
7. What has been the hardest thing for you?
8. What would you wish to do about passing on the historical identity/trauma?
9. What support and what kind of support would you need to enlist in order to accomplish this?

AFTERWORD
Affirmation & Reflection in Facilitation Skills

In 2021, my colleagues joined me in conducting a research study to evaluate the co-vision process. Using mixed methodology, we investigated to determine if participants experienced more self-compassion and well-being after their involvement with co-vision. Fifteen participants from our monthly co-vision groups volunteered to form their own smaller groups to facilitate bi-monthly, alternating between a listening circle and a compassionate witnessing circle, for a total of 18 circles over nine months.

It became apparent that facilitation skills needed special attention in both the questioning and the ability to stay present to the storyteller. Facilitators needed more skill-building to support regulating their own emotional space and that of their groups. It was apparent that facilitators needed reinforcement in the way they created the safe spaces for sharing, and help in refraining from "fixing" the storyteller's dilemma. The solution to this would be to provide more practice and feedback in working between the landscape of events and the landscape of identity. After some reflection on how to create a systemic model for supporting facilitators, our co-visioning colleagues introduced an approach for those new to the process to practice the facilitation questions that scaffold, externalize, and zigzag from landscape of events to the landscape of identity.

Here are helpful guidelines in establishing a foundation for facilitators to have greater sensitivity when listening to a story without being distracted with the details of the story or attempting to problem solve. Providing potential facilitators with at least three months to meet for monthly practice in dyads using the exercises in Appendix C. Facilitators would commit to practicing the Exercise 1 as suggested for three weeks with different family, friends, and colleagues following the initial session. The second meeting of facilitators would be spent reflecting on what was useful and what improvements could be made in order to refine their own awareness. Following this reflection, Exercise 2 (as in Appendix C) would be introduced. The same procedure for practicing with others would be assigned after the session.

In the third month the final Exercise 3 is introduced. The process is repeated again. At the end of three months of working in dyads, practicing each exercise set of questions with others, then reflecting on their experiences, we are ready to have the facilitators use compassionate witnessing and listening circles with a level of competence and the ability to regulate their own and others' emotions. Seven to eight participants should be the maximum number in a small circle. Inviting the fundamentals of narrative voice into a circle must always be a well normed space. Facilitators should remind themselves continually of the acronym, S.P.A.R.K.

Guide for Facilitators:

S - Safe spaces: Meet at a regular time each month to enjoy company with others.

P - Passions: Choose topics and interests or hobbies that are close to participants' hearts.

A - Attract fun: Make check-ins and check-outs fun and invite laughter and exploration that makes meaningful connections.

R - Rebellious: Step out and try something different at times.

K - Keep doing it: Remember to keep affirming each other using the 5 Cs (Connect, Compassion, Curious, enCourage and Community).

PROCESS: Affirmation & Reflection Dyads for Training Facilitators

1. Check-in with a fun fact.

2. Describe the norms for the affirmation circle. **Role play the process for the large group.**

3. Divide the group into dyads.

4. Give 30 minutes for each dyad. Each dyad chooses who will be the facilitator and the presenter or storyteller.
   a. Facilitator asks the presenter specific questions from the exercise.
   b. Dyads have reflection time to write.
   c. Dyad shares writings, starting with the facilitator.

5. Large Group Check-In: What did you learn, realize or were surprised by during the interaction exercise?

The process is repeated and the roles are switched.

Facilitation Dyad Practice

1. The group is asked to work in dyads. A facilitator will practice the questions below.

2. A presenter will engage with their own experience in sharing.
   a. 15 minutes for the questions is given.
   b. Silent reflection of writing for five minutes for both parties
   c. Followed by 10 minutes of acknowledgments starting with the facilitator, then the presenter

3. After each 30 minutes, we will gather in a large group for a check-in.

4. Then a second round of dyads will engage in the same process but swap roles.

Afterword

The process of compassionate witnessing will contain four segments:

1. **Dialogue:** The facilitator asks a person the questions designed from the Exercise 1 to 3. (15 minutes)

2. **Reflection Time:** Each member quietly writes a reflection paragraph. No conversation. (5 minutes)

    a. **Facilitator's prompt:** Acknowledge the gifts the person presenting gave you and the values or traits you were privileged to experience with them.

    b. **Presenter's prompt:** What did you get in touch with as you spoke? What experiences have built resilience in you and why? Are these strengths and/or challenges?

3. **Affirmation Time:** Facilitator and presenter acknowledge participation (5 minutes)

    a. The facilitator shares the acknowledgment about the competences (gifts).

    b. The presenter thanks the facilitator and shares the personal reflection paragraph.

4. **Feedback:** Large group gathers for a meta-conversation. **Question:** What did you learn, realize, or were surprised by during that interaction? (15 minutes)

PROCESS
Dialogue 1

- Facilitator asks the chosen questions.
- Remember to ask extended questions in between, e.g. how, what, whose, and why.
- Remain neutral and curious.

Reflection 2 (Quiet reflection to write)

- This must be in total silence. Dyads follow the prompts in writing a paragraph.
- No advice should be given.

- Writing responses are in words and phrases the person has used.
- Be respectful of the person's story.

Affirmation 3 (dialogue)

- The facilitator responds by sharing what he/she has written.
- The presenter starts by thanking the facilitator and then shares the reflection with the facilitator.
- What did you connect with?
- Why?
- Where is this taking you now?

Feedback Large gathering 4 (all participants)

- What was that like for the presenter to share?
- How did you feel as the facilitator?
- Open the discussion to the group for any further challenges?
- Comment on where you felt a shift happen.
- What was it that made the shift?

PLEASE NOTE:

1. This process may be repeated with the dyads switching roles.

2. The "take it back" ethic applies. Each colleague is committed to try the set of questions out with someone each week before the next month's co-vision meeting.

3. This repetition helps to ground facilitators in their skills with externalizing an issue, the scaffolding process of questioning, and the ability to move into the landscape of identity more easily. It should become second nature in their facilitation.

Appendix C provides additional exercises for facilitation groups. Learning to work with affirmations and reflections around specific trauma such as historical trauma can support communities in building a positive culture that welcomes diversity.

Resources

Bailie, J. W. (2019). A science of human dignity: Belonging, voice and agency as universal human needs. *IIRP Presidential Paper Series, 1*, 1-16. https://www.iirp.edu/pps1

Brown, B. (2015). *Rising strong: How the ability to reset transforms the way we live, love, parent, and lead.* Random House.

Costello, B., Wachtel, J., & Wachtel, T. (2019). *Restorative circles in schools: Building community and enhancing learning* (2nd ed.). International Institute for Restorative Practices.

Duvall, J., & Beres, L. (2011). *Innovations in narrative therapy: Connecting practice, training, and research.* W. W. Norton.

Freedman, J., & Combs, G. (1996). *Narrative therapy: The social construction of preferred realities.* W. W. Norton.

Harari, Y. N. (2019). *21 Lessons for the 21st century.* Spiegel & Grau.

Levine, P. A. (2015). *Trauma and memory: Brain and body in a search for the living past.* North Atlantic Books.

Morgan, A. (2000). *What is narrative therapy? An easy-to-read introduction.* Dulwich Centre Publications.

Picoult, J. (2013). *The storyteller: A novel.* Washington Square Press.

Porges, S. W. (2011). *The polyvagal theory: Neurophysiological foundations of emotions, attachment, communication, and self-regulation.* W. W. Norton.

Rundell, F. C. (2021, Summer). Processing trauma using the Relational Care Ladder. *IIRP Presidential Paper Series, 4*, 1-20. https://www.iirp.edu/pps4

Rundell, F. C. (2022). *Systemic racism: A transgenerational trauma haunting the soul of South Africa*. Samuel DeWitt Proctor Institute for Leadership, Equity, & Justice. https://proctor.gse.rutgers.edu/sites/default/files/SystemicRacism_SA_0.pdf

Rundell, F. C., Sheety, A., & Negrea, V. (2018). Managing trauma: A restorative process. In E. Sengupta & P. Blessinger (Eds.), *Refugee education: Integration and acceptance of refugees in mainstream education* (pp. 17-31). Emerald Publishing. https://doi.org/10.1108/S2055-364120180000011004

Rundell, F. C. (2001). *Co-vision: A community program for caring professionals* [Unpublished doctoral dissertation]. University of Zululand.

Safran, J. D., & Muran, J. C. (2000). *Negotiating the therapeutic alliance: A relational treatment guide*. Guilford Press.

Sheety, A., & Rundell, F. (2012). A PLG (professional learning group): How to stimulate learners' engagement in problem-solving. *US-China Education Review, 2*(5), 497-503.

Tomm, K. (1988). Interventive interviewing: Part III. Intending to ask lineal, circular, reflexive and strategic questions? *Family Process, 27*, 1–15.

Wachtel, T. (2016). *Defining restorative*. International Institute for Restorative Practices. https://www.iirp.edu/images/2022/WachtelDefiningRestorative2016.pdf

Weingarten, K. (2003). *Common shock: Witnessing violence every day — how we are harmed, how we can heal*. Dutton.

White, M. (1989). The externalizing of the problem and the re-authoring of lives and relationships. *Dulwich Centre Newsletter, 3*(2), 3-21.

White, M. (2007). *Maps of narrative practice*. W. W. Norton.

Made in United States
North Haven, CT
29 April 2024